$\mathcal{A}$CKNOWLEDGEMENTS

 I wish to recognize several people who have contributed greatly to this work:

All of the authors. Thanks for sharing your gifts.

Dixon Smith who is my partner and friend.

Penny Pence Smith, Dixon's wife who inspires us to think and rethink our mission.

Mary Ann Weatherman who is the finest copy editor I have ever worked with. She helps writers say what they intend to say.

Michael Josephson my friend and teacher, and the rest of the staff at the Josephson Institute of Ethics.

John Martin at the Character Education Partnership who helps keep everyone focused on the mission.

David Wangaard from The School For Ethical Education. Your insights continue to challenge me. I look forward to our growing friendship and joint professional efforts.

My mother and father, Nell and T.A. Vincent who continue to inspire me on a daily basis.

Cynthia Vincent, my wife, companion, friend and mother of our daughter Mary Kathryn. I could not travel around the country and work with schools and school districts without your support. You truly are the wings beneath my feet.

Mary Kathryn Vincent, my daughter. May you stay forever young.

ONTENTS

 **Dedication**

This book is dedicated to Kevin Ryan, Thomas Lickona, Sandy McDonnell, Linda McKay and Jerry Corley, and last but not least Michael Josephson. The nation owes you a debt of gratitude.

Promising Practices in

CHARACTER
EDUCATION

NINE SUCCESS STORIES
FROM AROUND THE COUNTRY

Edited by Dr. Philip Fitch Vincent
Foreword by Dr. Kevin Ryan

Promising Practices in
CHARACTER
EDUCATION

NINE SUCCESS STORIES
FROM AROUND THE COUNTRY

Edited by Dr. Philip Fitch Vincent
Foreword by Dr. Kevin Ryan

Produced and published by
CHARACTER DEVELOPMENT GROUP

Cover design by Paul Turley
Book design by Dixon J. Smith & Paul Turley

ISBN 0-9653163-0-0 12.00

FOREWORD

Dr. Kevin Ryan

 Is character education the American school's latest fad or its oldest mission?" The answer to the question is "Yes" and "Yes." The schools in Colonial America were brought into being out of concern for the moral lives of children. Parents in the frontier towns and villages of the New World were acutely aware that their children were cut off from the civilized and the "civilizing" world they had left behind in Europe. The first public schools in the New World were started in Massachusetts. In 1647 the state legislature passed the *Old Deluder Satan Act* requiring towns of a certain size to establish schools. In turn, the schools were to teach children to read the Bible, thus gaining the moral strength to resist the temptations of Satan. As the colonies transformed themselves into the world's first modern democracy, the new nation's schools were seen as an important means for the education of citizens. The writings of the Founding Fathers are filled with the statements about the need to educate people to the moral responsibilities required of democratic self-government. Our founders were convinced that their fledgling nation rested on personal virtues and strong moral character. And, while over the years the public schools have put aside the religious basis for moral and character education, the need has persisted to educate children and new Americans to the moral responsibilities of good citizenship and a fruitful personal life. Or, at least, it persisted until recent decades.

The United States of the twentieth century is a vast and varied continental nation. We are a stew of many races, religions, national and regional origins. Our very size and variety has forced upon us a commitment to a set of civic values, moral values which are the nation's social glue. Among these core values are concern for the weak and the underdog, a passion for liberty, a respect for freedom of religion, a belief in personal responsibility, and love of our country and its traditions. A key element in our national value system has been our devotion to public education, a devotion which stems in large part from the belief that our schools are an essential means to convey our binding and shared values to the young. Our children are expected to learn what it is to be a good American, a good citizen, in both the form and the substance of our schools. And, in general, that was the way education occurred until the late 1960s.

In a few short years, the nation experienced a civil rights revolution which brought long-simmering racial tensions to the light, an ugly and divisive war in Southeast Asia, a sexual revolution which seemingly overnight changed the sexual attitudes and behavior of millions, and an explosion of drug use. All of this happened in a matter of four or five years and the effect was to destroy the widely held sense that Americans were bound by a common set of values. In fact, the perception was that we were spinning apart, that the American moral consensus was shattered. The social glue was dissolving.

America's two million teachers were just as confused as everyone else, particularly since they were on the front lines of much of the turmoil over racial issues, drugs, the new sexuality and war protest. And while no one announced from the State House or the local board of education that teachers were no longer required to teach our civic values, nevertheless, many teachers stepped back. Confused and disoriented themselves by all the social change and controversy, many teachers, often with the encouragement of the universities and educational spokesmen, abandoned their responsibilities to teach our core moral and ethical values. They, of course, had their own moral values, but they kept them to themselves and, in effect, became information technicians. They delivered information, but gave the arena of moral values and character formation wide berth.

While there is still some scar-tissue on the American psyche left from the Sixties, by and large, the values upheaval is over and the consensus has been restored. Indeed, there is an almost desperate search to reach social equilibrium. Much of the energy behind this search comes from the frightening statistics about youth crime and pathology. In the last thirty years we have seen a four hundred percent rise in out-of-wedlock births largely by teenage mothers. Youth suicides and homicides have increased in similar proportions. As a nation, we are deeply worried about our young and the way in which the adult community is preparing them for their own adulthood. As one major Washington politician said recently, "We have twelve-year olds having babies; fifteen-year olds killing one another; seventeen year olds dying of AIDS; and eighteen-year olds graduating from high school unable to read."

In the face of the frightening statistics of youth violence and disorder and the personal experiences of many people, the public is turning to schools for help. From the White House to the housing project calls for help are being heard, calls for teachers to demand better behavior from students and help children gain the strong good habits needed for a civil society.

In effect, people are rediscovering the obvious, inevitable fact that teachers and schools have children from the time they are four or five until their late teens. This is the time in their lives when their moral values and habits are formed. This is the time when their characters are like soft wax, capable of forming themselves into strong, virtuous individuals or weak, disordered menaces to themselves and those around them. But during the years that these pleas for a return to moral and character education became louder and more insistent, American educators had a different agenda, one encompassed by school restructuring and reform, by Goals 2000 and attempts to raise academic achievement.

The retreat of the schools from moral and character education following the tumult of the Sixties was not a complete rout. Thousands and thousands of teachers still "kept the faith," but for the most part this topic slipped out of sight in the American schools. Nevertheless, a handful of University-based educational theorists and researchers explored ways for schools to engage students in the moral life. The decades of the 1970s and 1980s were a time of much intellectual ferment. Neo-Deweyians argued with Neo-Durkheimians; traditionalist argued with cognitive moral developmentalists; and on and on. Except for the much denounced "values clarification movement," the schools were largely untouched by these academic debates and squabbles. The author, a minor warrior in these ivory tower battles, had a conversation with the late Lawrence Kohlberg, one of the leading theorists, shortly before his death in the late 1980s. The upshot of the exchange was, "One of these days the schools are going to turn and ask us how to get back to moral and character education and we aren't near to being ready!" In the last few years, teachers and administrators, encouraged by parents and community leaders, have been clamoring for direction and for concrete suggestions on how to "do" moral and character education. But in the midst of a full-voiced call back to character education, what practitioners are hearing from the researchers and theorists has been largely more theories and more research. However, that is not the entire story.

During the last several years, practicing educators across the country have been working to reclaim the moral mission of the schools. Quietly and largely unnoticed, individual schools and districts have put together programs and initiatives for real children in real classrooms. Sometimes theory-based, sometime not, these innovators have sorted through the literature and the research and developed their own pragmatic solutions to the problems and the potentials of their students. This book is testimony to their efforts and their successes. The book is a set of stories needing to be told.

The collector and editor of these tales, Philip Fitch Vincent, deserves special recognition. He represents what has been lacking in the efforts to return our schools to their historic mission of character education. He is both a theorist and a practitioner; both a scholar and a teacher; both a thinker and a doer. As educators grope to address the moral needs of our children, we need a vision of what character and moral education look like in the context of these places we call schools. We need models to help us direct and focus our efforts, *Promising Practices in Character Education—Nine Success Stories from Around the Country* fills this void. Phil Vincent knows children; he knows schools; and he knows his theory. As this book demonstrates, he also knows how to put them all together in a set of fascinating stories.

Kevin Ryan
Center for the Advancement of Ethics and Character, Boston University
June, 1996

NTRODUCTION

Dr. Philip Fitch Vincent

In sharing with a colleague that I needed to write an introduction to the anthology, *Promising Practices in Character Education*, I explained how authors in eight school districts described their procedures in developing and implementing character education programs. Enthused with excitement from the positive effects of these character education programs, he rapidly assessed the situation, "Phil, keep your introduction short. In light of all the wonderful things occurring in these school districts, you want your readers to be able to quickly get to each school's unfoldment."

With the exception of Chip Wood's insightful overview concerning the "Responsive Classroom," each chapter in *Promising Practices in Character Education* is the story of one school or one school district and its efforts to develop the character of its students. Each story is inspiring, while offering practical insights into the steps needed to forge a character education project. Perhaps one story will not provide you with all of the answers you are seeking. Keep reading. The odds are good that the next one or the one after it might.

Character education is a grassroots movement evolving across the nation. The unification of theory and practice indicate the seriousness of its efforts. From higher learning, proponents such as Thomas Lickona, Kevin Ryan, and James Leming have provided excellent historical background information and examples of solid pedagogy for character educators to consider.

From the schools, leaders such as Henry Hoffman, Rudolfo Bernardo, Sharon Banas, Helen LeGette and others included in this collection have inspired their peers in the practical steps needed to move theory into practice in implementing a character education program.

John Martin from the Character Education Partnership and Michael Josephson from "Character Counts" and the Josephson Institute of Ethics have played major roles in facilitating moral cognizance in communities by helping their members recognize the importance that good character plays in the life of the community.

From my travels and work with school districts around the country, I have observed several practices which seem to be apparent in all successful or emerging character education programs. Individuals involved in character education do not see this as a fad nor an "add-on" program, unless a school or community has decided to do "character lite." This is represented by practices such as the purchase of a packaged program which is used once or twice a week or the reading of "inspiring" stories over the intercom for five minutes each day. Programs such as these are doomed to fail. It is apparent to serious practitioners that developing character is not easy. A character education program worthy of its name reflects the ethos or life of the school. It occurs throughout the entire day. Character education two times a week or five minutes a day requires minimal buy-in and effort on the part of the community and the school. It will produce, at the best, minimal results.

The consistency of each school or school district's efforts in emphasizing similar character practices helps develop the character of its students. These common characteristics may include the development of good social exercises which are learned through practice; cooperative learning for all students; literature which highlights good character; teaching for thinking; and the promotion of service learning.

Some character education programs will have strong district leadership. Others will depend on each school, through site-based decision making, developing its distinctive character education program. Although

I prefer a strong district presence to insure consistency, I am aware that one outstanding school can influence by example the direction of many other schools within a district.

It is also gratifying to learn that communities can come to an agreement on the character traits which should be accented in each school or school district. Many districts, with community emphasis, have chosen character traits which strongly resemble the Six Pillars of Character of the Josephson Institute of Ethics: Trustworthiness, Respect, Responsibility, Caring, Fairness and Citizenship. Others have used honesty instead of trustworthiness. Still others have added traits such as perseverance or courage. Most important, though, is the consensus in all communities on the selection of these character traits, suggesting that community members realize that character is not a racial or socioeconomic issue. This supports the notion that good character and its development is valuable for all.

In conclusion, the Character Development Group is committed to its role of providing support to schools and districts nationwide. It is our belief that our training preparations and publications such as *Promising Practices in Character Education* help fulfill our goal. Good luck in your efforts to make character education a reality in your school or school district. Keep us informed so we educators can keep the training wheels turning on promising practices in character education!

Philip Vincent

1 BURLINGTON, NC

Character Education in the Burlington City Schools Helps Students

Dr. Helen LeGette

Assistant Superintendent,
Burlington City Schools

 ## History

In recent years, school personnel have seen more disrespectful and aggressive acts among students. At both the local and national levels, juvenile crime rates have increased, and issues such as substance abuse and sexual promiscuity continue to be problems. Because of the very high number of single-parent homes and the number of working mothers, many youngsters have large amounts of unsupervised time and are therefore susceptible to potentially negative influences of peers and the media. The influence of the family and the church on the moral development of children has declined, and the messages conveyed in an alarming number of television programs, movies, and rap music lyrics glorify antisocial behavior and desensitize the viewers.

In Burlington (and in school systems across the nation), programs such as drug-abuse education and pregnancy prevention are and have been in place to address some of the above trends. Despite the modest success of such programs, they address the *symptoms* rather than the *causes* of the troubling trends in student behavior. Therefore, it has become increasingly clear to parents and educators alike that schools cannot be values-neutral. This realization led local school and community representatives to come together to lay the foundation for the Character Education Project.

Taking the position that schools cannot afford to be "moral by-standers" (Thomas Lickona, *Educating for Character),* the school system convened the Character Education Committee in July, 1994. Committee members included school personnel (teachers, administrators, counselors, and the chairman of the board of education), the editors of the two area newspapers, several ministers, a city council member, and representatives of the following community agencies: Burlington Police Department, Department of Social Services, Alamance Coalition Against Drug Abuse, Burlington Housing Authority, Alamance Coalition on Adolescent Pregnancy, and the Salvation Army Boys and Girls Clubs. (The associate superintendent chaired the committee and has continued to coordinate the project, as well as serving as what Dr. Henry Huffman calls the "executive champion" of the character education initiative.)

At their first meeting, the Character Education Committee discussed disturbing changes they had observed in youthful behavior and attitudes, and they reviewed some of the influences leading to those changes. This diverse group was immediately united on one critical issue: concern about the youth in Burlington. At a subsequent meeting, members responded to the open-ended item, "I want *my children* to be…" or "I want *our students* to be…" The committee then discussed their individual lists of desirable character traits in small groups and compiled lists of common traits.

After this activity, the whole group came together to attempt to agree on which principles of character would be desirable for *all* students in the school system. The committee rather quickly reached consensus that the six pillars of character promoted by the Character Counts Coalition (trustworthiness, responsibility, respect, fairness, caring, and citizenship) represented the qualities they wished to instill in local students. Following further discussion, they adopted those six traits as the Burlington City Schools Principles of Character which would be integrated into the curriculum at all levels.

To introduce the project to the schools and to the community, the school system contracted with Dr. Henry Huffman, a national leader in character education, to conduct an awareness session for committee members, administrators, board of education members and selected teachers and counselors in August, 1994. Dr. Huffman followed up with nine hours of additional instruction for elementary teachers on ways to integrate character education into the curriculum. In that workshop, teachers developed a reading-resource list for character education. That list identified literary works for each grade level (kindergarten through fifth grade) which were already included in the curriculum and could be used to teach the principles of character. Workshop participants also generated numerous ideas for student projects at various grade levels.

At the opening convocation in August, 1994, Dr. Huffman addressed the entire school "family" on the responsibilities which *all* school employees share in the character development of children. In the ensuing weeks, teachers who were involved in Dr. Huffman's workshops shared information and ideas with their colleagues in the individual schools. The associate superintendent also met with several faculties and the local Parent–Teacher Association (PTA) Council to discuss the project.

In a cooperative effort between the school system and the Turrentine Middle School PTA, Dr. Philip Vincent, author of *Developing Character in Students,* conducted an optional two-hour awareness session for middle and high school personnel, and that evening he held a public session for parents. In June, 1995, Dr. Vincent came back to Burlington to conduct a two-day workshop on integrating character education into the middle and high school curriculums. Participants in that workshop developed action plans for their schools, which they shared in building-level workshops when school opened in August. Dr. Vincent returned to conduct additional in-service activities for elementary personnel in January, 1996, and for middle and secondary personnel in February, 1996.

In October, 1995, Rachel Ostreicher-Bernheim, president of the Raoul Wallenberg Committee, and Dr. Kathleen Morin, who wrote the *Raoul Wallenberg: A Study of Heroes* curriculum, conducted awareness sessions for administrators and counselors on that material. Ms. Bernheim and Dr. Morin also led workshops for elementary and middle school personnel on using the lives of real heroes to teach good character. (The school system purchased sets of *The Study of Heroes* materials for all elementary and middle schools.)

The school system also secured a number of other resources to help teachers integrate character education into the curriculum. Among these were the curriculum kits prepared by the Heartwood Institute, which utilize award-winning children's literature to foster character development, and the *Working Together* kits (American Guidance Services, Inc.), which use folk tales for the same purpose. In addition, central office personnel have compiled and disseminated various resource lists on character education for teachers and counselors. To promote further interest in the project, the school system purchased copies of *Developing Character in Students* for all certified personnel. Also, every administrator, counselor and board of education member received an individual copy of *Educating for Character,* by Thomas Lickona.

 ## Current Activities

System-wide activities have provided a foundation for the project and equipped school personnel with the knowledge, skills, and resources needed to integrate character education into the curriculum. Building-level committees have developed plans for individual schools, and parent committees and community members have also assisted in promoting project activities. At the building level, the implementation plans have certain commonalities, but the activities vary from school to school.

For example, most schools begin the day—or at least every assembly—with the Pledge of Allegiance. In several elementary schools, students who have been recognized for displaying good character lead "morning exercises" over the intercom, which include the Pledge and a patriotic song. During this time, the principal or counselor may give a brief lesson on character, recognize students for their behavior, or announce student or staff birthdays for the day.

Special assemblies and other events focus on patriotism and good citizenship. All elementary schools have developed incentive plans to recognize students for displaying behavior which reflects the principles of character. At Eastlawn Elementary School, for instance, students who are "caught being good" have their pictures displayed in the cafeteria. The citizens of the month at Andrews Elementary School are treated to lunch at a local restaurant. At Grove Park, the good citizens ride to the restaurant in a limousine provided by a parent! Students at Newlin Elementary School use their weekly closed-circuit television program to highlight good citizenship, and Hillcrest Elementary students produce bimonthly puppet shows on the featured principle of character.

The Terrific Kids program is correlated with the character traits in most of the elementary schools. This offers public recognition for good character and provides a means for all students, regardless of their academic ability, to be honored. All schools have some form of student recognition program, such as Williams High School's "Best of the Bull-dogs," a designation for which teachers may nominate students for their acts of kindness or respect.

In all schools, the character traits are posted in classrooms. Bulletin boards in halls and cafeterias also focus on character. Teachers use lesson materials to lead discussions on honesty, respect and responsibility. Counselors reinforce these principles in periodic classroom guidance activities. In discipline conferences with students and parents, administrators take advantage of the "teachable moment" also.

Every school has participated in several service projects which help to integrate *caring* into the school environment. To illustrate, a fifth grade class at Hillcrest Elementary decorated the homeless shelter for Christmas and helped to make cookies for the guests there; Cummings High School's academically gifted students "adopted" handicapped students for a joint re-search project; Turrentine Middle School conducted a school-wide project ("Walk a Mile for Their Shoes") and raised approximately $3,000 to buy shoes for needy school children; and almost every school conducted some type of food drive for the hungry during 1994-95. Many additional school and community service projects are planned for the 1995-96 school year.

Character education has also become a vehicle for teaching students to understand different cultures. The entire staff and student body at Smith Elementary School joined in a special project, "Around the World in 180 Days," based on the Heartwood materials. During the 1995-96 school year, every student and staff member at Hillcrest Elementary will be involved in a "freedom quilt" project coordinated by the art teacher. Cultural diversity training and workshops on peer mediation and conflict reso-lution have been offered in several schools, and peer mediators are active at the elementary and middle school levels.

Recognizing the truth in William Bennett's observation that "there is nothing more influential, more determinant, in a child's life than the moral power of quiet example" (*The Book of Virtues*, p. 11), the school system has emphasized the importance of the staff's modeling good char-acter in all interactions with students.

Also, motivational speeches by Clebe McClary, a Vietnam war hero; Astronaut Lt. Col. Bill McArthur; Lorenzo Romar, former professional basketball player; and Willie Horton, professional baseball player, have helped reinforce the importance of good character to students. To involve parents directly in the project, each elementary PTA distributed a locally developed resource, "Character Education: Suggestions for Parents," which outlines ways that parents can instill good character in their children.

All of the activities are intended to help students "know the good, desire the good and do the good," as advocated by Thomas Lickona. Lessons may focus on respect, caring, etc., but the real test is the students' demonstration of their understanding through application. Therefore, the schools provide many opportunities for students to show fairness and consideration for others and to exhibit responsible behavior. Because character education is a way of life rather than an "add-on," no additional staff is required. However, the commitment of the entire staff is critical to the success of the project.

 ## Evaluation

Obviously, true changes in character take place over time and are difficult to quantify. Being mindful of the adage that "not every thing that counts can be counted and not every thing that can be counted counts," personnel in Burlington have not allowed evaluation to drive the Character Education Project. However, the staff did conduct an informal evaluation in November, 1995. Because the project is in only its second year, rather limited results were anticipated.

To evaluate initial progress, the associate superintendent requested that elementary teachers respond to an anonymous four-item survey, on which they answered questions as to whether they had observed changes in school climate or differences in student behavior. They also were asked to share their thoughts regarding comments about the project that they had heard from parents or other teachers, and to offer suggestions for strengthening local efforts to promote good character and citizenship. Administrators at all levels were invited to respond to the survey as well. (The teacher survey was limited to the elementary level, because the major focus of the project was on the elementary schools during 1994-95.) The response rate for teachers was 78 percent, with 149 of 192 teachers and counselors returning the surveys, while 28 administrators responded.

In response to Item 1, the majority of teachers (70 percent) indicated that they had noticed a positive difference in school climate since the project began. (Almost 15 percent stated that they were new to the school system and could not make a comparison.) The following are sample comments from teachers: "Students are more aware of good manners. Many now say 'excuse me,' and this is a terrific change." "Yes! The children are more polite to each other. They are very aware that 'good manners' are important. Not only are the children more courteous; the staff is too!" "Children are connecting the way they are treated with the way they treat others."

Administrators' assessments followed a similar pattern, with 18 of 28 respondents checking "yes" to the item regarding changes in school climate. Seventeen of the administrators (61 percent) noted improvements in student behavior. Explaining further, they commented: "Students and staff appear to make more conscious efforts to be helpful and considerate"; "Character education has created a unity of purpose"; and "Teachers commented from the beginning that [character education] was long overdue. They have wholeheartedly supported the project."

When asked whether they had noticed a difference in student attitudes or behavior, one administrator observed that "There are fewer disciplinary problems, and students are getting better at solving their own problems."

Answering the same question, 77 teachers indicated that they had seen differences. Only 15 (10 percent) replied that they had not yet observed differences in student behavior. Sample comments from teachers revealed: "Kids are taking more responsibility for their actions"; "Children are more inclined to come up with resolutions rather than arguing or fighting"; and "I have often heard students recognize certain behaviors of students and identify those with character traits. For example, 'What she did was very responsible.'"

The third survey item asked respondents to share comments they had heard from teachers, students or parents about the Character Education Project. Once again, the responses were very positive. A teacher revealed, "One parent who heard the morning exercises stated, 'Schools should do more of this.' The teacher added, "All the comments I have heard have been very positive. Teachers and parents seem very pleased that the school is working on character."

Another offered, "Teachers and parents are very grateful and supportive of this program. I personally think that in today's society this program is very much needed. For some kids, this is the only time they hear these words and the thoughts behind the words." "Our staff and parents feel this is a positive influence on our children," stated one administrator. Another participant noted overhearing a teacher say, "Because of [this] project, students seem more willing to be helpers and friends to one another, no matter what race, age, sex, or ability level."

The final survey item asked for suggestions to strengthen the school system's efforts to promote good character (citizenship). The most common recommendations included seeking ways to involve parents to a greater extent in reinforcing the principles of character at home, increasing the amount of publicity about the project to the community, and providing more assemblies and other opportunities to present positive role models for the students.

When reviewing evaluation results of a character education project, it is very important to understand that character education is not a *program* that can easily be reduced to numbers. It is a way of behaving and relating to others, and it is reflected in the daily lives of students and staff members. Simply stated, character education is a conscious, cooperative effort to refocus on basic, universal principles of character which are critical to the survival of civilized society. Its true effects will be revealed in countless, subtle acts of kindness, respect and responsibility.

 ## Future Plans

Because the Character Education Project is a relatively new effort in Burlington, the immediate goal is to continue to integrate the principles of character throughout the curriculum. Staff development activities, faculty meetings and committee planning sessions will provide opportunities for teachers and counselors to share ideas and to develop further resources for use in the classroom. As new teachers are hired, they will have opportunities to learn about character education and will be encouraged to integrate character development into their instructional programs.

Classroom and community activities promoting character education will continue, and the staff will be encouraged to seek new avenues for student participation in service-learning projects. In several schools, teachers have identified character education goals as part of their own professional development plans, and they will implement those plans at the building level. System wide efforts to enhance community awareness of the project will continue through media coverage and presentations to civic and church groups. A major thrust will be to enlist the help of parents and other community and agency personnel in reinforcing the principles of character. An overriding goal is to have Burlington's schools, families, churches and community organizations unite efforts to develop good character in their children and youth.

2 ST. LOUIS, MO

An Active Partnership Between School, Home and Community Defines the Personal Responsibility Education Process —The Largest Community Experiment in Character Education

Diane Stirling

A simulation game in Arctic Survival that illustrates economic concepts generates a discussion of initiative and perseverance...

Second graders reading *Molly's Pilgrim* talk about how feelings are spared with discretion...

Middle school students cut commercials for "Respect" at a professional sound studio...

Seniors spend the day with professionals from diverse fields as they learn an ethical decision-making process and apply it to dilemmas that confront people on the job...

Third graders award "expressions of character" that they see in their classmates...

Elementary students listen as a storyteller enacts a tale of courage...

High school students rehab an inner-city home in a student-driven project that is part of a community service course.

This brief collection offers a glimpse of character education in a few of the more than 390 public schools that dot a three-county region of the St. Louis metropolitan area. The varied experiences share common roots, originating in the Personal Responsibility Education Process (PREP). A project of the Cooperating School Districts, PREP involves the voluntary participation of 30 public school districts, including more than 13,000 teachers and 213,000 students.

Considered the largest experiment in character education in the country, PREP serves as a model for school systems and communities throughout the United States and as far away as Hong Kong, Mexico and Denmark. As a model, it is not what PREP does, but how it does it that matters. The hallmarks of its operations are building consensus, stimulating grass roots innovation, and sharing resources. They were built into the system by the founders.

How It All Began

Sanford McDonnell, chairman emeritus of McDonnell Douglas Corporation and a catalyst in the arena of business ethics, focused his attention on youth in the late 1980s. He represented a corporate community that was willing to invest both financially and personally in effective character education. McDonnell saw public schools as a starting place, the fulcrum of a metropolitan response that recognizes the essential role of home, school and community in passing values onto our children. He enlisted the partnership of Cooperating School Districts (CSD), an educational consortium founded in 1928 that provides staff development, leadership and support services to public schools in 46 districts.

In 1987, Sanford McDonnell, CSD administrators and seven superintendents explored how to implement character education. Recognizing that they could not prescribe a set of values or a "one size fits all" solution, the superintendents sought the flexibility to develop approaches that fit the needs and contexts of their school communities. Their respective staff members worked together in developing a workable structure. This group laid the groundwork for a process that provides support, resources and guidance, yet allows a high degree of autonomy and generates grass-roots involvement. They committed their districts to develop character education over five years with three criteria.

They would:

1. invest heavily in training and staff development;
2. sustain successful initiatives resulting from their research; and
3. share these concepts with others.

At the end of that period, a reservoir of field-tested ideas for grades K-12 was available to other districts, as well as a proven method of consensus-building that brought members of the community together to identify and define the character traits the schools would emphasize.

 ## Building Consensus

"PREP does not promote one set of values," McDonnell says. "It gives schools a process that lets them rediscover their own values and reinforce them." An eight-step approach integrates character education into a school's philosophy, mission and policies, its curricula, student experiences, staff development and budget. The focal point of the process is a list of character traits identified and defined through a consensus-building approach. This procedure has been honed by the collective experience of district participants who have guided their communities through it. A model, based on their most effective efforts, includes the following steps:

Identify the players
Adults in closest contact with students define, teach and model the character traits. These people—parents; teachers; counselors; administrators; local business, religious and civic leaders; bus drivers; secretaries; cooks; nurses; custodial workers; librarians; volunteers and involved members of the community—are invited to participate in selecting traits the district and each of its schools will emphasize.

Allow time for reflection
The invitation asks these individuals to reflect on the traits that enrich their lives and then commit their thoughts to writing. What gives them a sense of meaningfulness, improves the community, and fosters the democratic principles of our country? What traits do they think can be effectively taught in a public school setting?

Meet

They bring this personal focus as they come together in a series of meetings or a single, day-long session to discuss character traits. They divide into teams and allow each member to share his or her written responses, preventing verbal high-rollers from dominating the conversations. The teams focus on a workable number (five or six) of traits, prioritize them, and develop a list that reflects the consensus of their team.

Coming together

The work of each group is reported and integrated into a collective list of traits. One technique reinforces this work visually as facilitators ask the groups to list each of their traits on separate cards. They then collect the cards and compile them, placing all those for "honesty" together on one part of the wall, those for "responsibility" in another area. The areas of agreement become readily apparent, allowing the group to reach a consensus on a list of desirable traits.

Wait

Time is provided to process what occurred. Participants are encouraged to talk among colleagues, friends and family. Additionally, feedback or dialogue sessions that allow them to voice their reactions is recommended.

Define the traits

A separate group, selected from group members involved in the first five steps, is developed to define the traits. These members are further divided into smaller units and each assigned the task of drafting definitions for one of the qualities. At this point, the dictionary and definitions other districts have developed provide a useful prototype.

Present the definitions for feedback

Definitions are presented in letters to be mailed to all participants. They may be published in newsletters and flyers, inviting people to react to them. Time is slotted for open meetings to air concerns and consider changes. Contention surrounding a particular trait or definition is eliminated, since the goal is to devise a list of traits that attracts universal support.

Integrate them into core policies and procedures

The traits and their definitions are incorporated into the mission statement of the school or district. They are visually reinforced through posters and displays in each building. A brochure is published and distributed which includes character expectations with established guidelines for each grade level.

Teach them to students

The words and definitions are introduced to students in the classroom by posting them and discussing their meaning in age-appropriate terms. Applications and actions that express the traits are discussed to familiarize students with the meaning of the words. As they see, hear and experience the traits, they gain the knowledge that allows the eventual integration of character education in their curriculum.

This model takes time—districts invest a year or more in the process—but it is worth it. The approach mitigates dissension with broad-based acceptance. "We did it this way, allowing the community within and around each school in the district to move through these steps," says B. R. Rhoads, principal of Bristol Elementary School in the Webster Groves School District. "It is not top-down management, but truly a collaborative process. As a result, teachers, parents and neighbors of the schools feel like stakeholders; they have ownership." They also have an understanding of consensus. "We learned that it has a lot to do with compromise. Our communities include right-wing groups, liberals and people who find themselves somewhere on the continuum between these poles," says Rhoads. "That the majority of our people feel comfortable and support our district's seven traits speaks to the power of consensus-building."

Grass-Roots Innovation

With a list of traits to anchor their efforts, educators tackle the challenge of how to introduce character education into daily learning. They find in PREP no formula or instruction manual, but guidelines that support their own needs assessment, imaginative program development, and risk-taking. The financial structure of the Cooperating School District's PREP project channels grant funds directly to those who conceive ways of teaching character education.

As a result, a math department chairman organized a two-day retreat for 25 teachers who incorporated goal-setting, perseverance, and an emphasis on mastery into the middle and high school curriculums. A district-wide team researched and wrote the Responsibility Education curriculum (K-8) based on ten character traits. Two high school social studies teachers developed a year-long course, Ethics in Science and Technology, to prepare seniors for issues they may face in their future careers. An elementary music curriculum committee cross-referenced nearly 400 songs by grade level and nine different traits, identifying cooperation, for example, with "Make New Friends," "The More We Get Together," and "Down by the Riverside." A suburban high school developed a leadership skills course. An art teacher selected folk tales that emphasized honesty and courage, and videotaped their telling for use throughout her district.

Original innovations are complemented in many schools with established character education curriculums. Programs from Quest International, the Jefferson Center for Character Education, Personality Fitness Training and MegaSkills, to suggest a few of those used by PREP schools, offer age-appropriate curricula, proven strategies, experienced trainers, skills training, class materials and ongoing support. The training components build the confidence of teachers and staff members in their ability to teach what the traits mean. Their curriculums and materials unify a school's efforts throughout the grade levels and provide a foundation from which to launch other initiatives.

The staff at Blades Elementary School, for instance, implemented the Jefferson Center's *Responsibility Skills: Lessons for Success* (Brooks,1990) and adapted the methods and skills to teach the district's traits. They went on to develop their own conflict-resolution training. As a result, students knew what they were talking about when they discussed self-control, discretion, cooperation, respect, responsible decision-making and compassion. These traits had become part of their knowledge base and required little explaining when introduced as attributes needed in mediation and conflict resolution. "This knowledge base is a prerequisite for integrating character education into daily learning," explains Dr. Jerry Corley, PREP Curriculum Integration coordinator for CSD.

Another prerequisite is the committed participation of teachers. One educator used an approach that not only involved her peers, but affirmed their confidence and dissolved their resistance to yet another reform. Josette Hochman, an English teacher and PREP coordinator at Parkway Central Middle School, took stock of what staff members had already done in the field. By identifying and sharing the strategies that were in place she demystified the concept, dissipated the fear that teachers would be burdened with add-on activities, and recognized that character education identifies aspects that have long been considered a part of good teaching. As she met one-on-one with teachers and counselors to document what they had accomplished, she built a foundation of trust. The staff responded with 100 percent participation in a series of consensus-building meetings that shaped an ambitious action plan for character education.

Sharing Ideas and Resources

Successful schools invest time in creating an acceptable comfort level. The leadership sets realistic expectations, devoting the first year to establishing a common language and visibly promoting the traits through signs, banners and brochures. Faculty and support staff explore creative ways to engage students, staff and parents with the words. Teachers are encouraged to experiment with new approaches, originate their own lessons and activities, invest time in related training, and look at what other schools are doing. The sharing of ideas and resources is critical at this stage of character education.

"If something works, teachers talk about it," says Tom Bick, director of pupil services as PREP coordinator for the Hazelwood district in St. Louis County. He indicates teachers' experiences carry more credibility than the most sophisticated sales pitch. Bick introduced a condensed version of the Lions–Quest *Skills for Growing* (1990) curriculum in a pilot project, a summer transition course preparing students for one of the district's two junior highs. The first session involved five staff members and 50 students in a two-week course. Teachers talked about the results and the next year the district's remaining junior high implemented the mini-course. Bick made sure Quest training was available to faculty throughout the district and watched as word of mouth generated interest that compounded each year. By 1995, more than 500 teachers had elected to take the training. The unabridged Lions–Quest curriculums became a familiar component of the regular school year.

Bick is continually in touch with teachers from each of his district's schools, creating avenues of exchange, sharing their innovations and experiences with others, scheduling staff-development opportunities, and connecting them with resources.

What Bick does within his district is magnified by CSD's PREP office, an administrative center that supports the work of 30 districts. Workshops and seminars showcasing experiments and advances of fellow teachers emanate from this hub. An annual national conference introduces leading authorities to hundreds of educators.

PREP also draws together a consortium of industry specialists, ethicists, educators and community leaders to advise teachers who are researching specific courses. Lectures and workshops provide resources for parents. A character education fair displays the districts' work to the general public. A library catalogues the progress within districts and offers resources to newcomers in character education through its volumes of original curriculums for elementary, middle and secondary schools. Guides for establishing an ethics course, a leadership skills class, a responsibility code and activities tailored to middle school advisory periods are available as well. Videos showing the mechanics of a successful recognition program, the dynamics of an Ethical Decision-Making workshop and the components of national character education curriculums are provided by the library, too.

 ## Evolving Toward Curriculum Integration

The three hallmarks of the PREP process—consensus, grass-roots innovation and sharing resources—create a firm foundation, stimulate growth and sustain it. The capacity to sustain commitment and investment allows character education to mature to the stage of curriculum integration.

"As character education develops within each community, we've watched it evolve from a series of projects and activities to a level where it is infused within the natural flow of academic learning," describes Linda McKay, CSD's director of PREP, who has nurtured the growth of the project since 1989.

Veteran districts that had progressed from a community consensus on the traits to a widespread familiarity with character education began to incorporate it into their curricula. They developed several tactics, from the formal revision of curricula to the ongoing adaptation of daily lessons. The St. Louis Public School District was one of the first to develop a process to incorporate character education perspectives into their curricula as they came up for scheduled review.

"We've found the more you approach these skills and values within the context of current events, science, math, health and literature, the greater the chance of assimilation," explains Superintendent Dr. David J. Mahan.

Other districts tackle the task by converting curricula for each grade level, one right after the other. Still others ask school staffs to re-examine their ongoing practices with an eye toward character education. McKay, a facilitator for many of these reviews, encourages schools to develop teams that include parents, teachers and non-teaching staff members. As the teams come together in a series of sessions or a half-day workshop, each group focuses on one particular trait and responds to specific questions: How are we going to bring a particular character trait into the life of our school? How can students see the word? How can they hear the word? How can they experience it? How can they act on it? Who can help us do this? What supplies do we need? What training do we need? How are we going to evaluate the results of these changes?

The questions continue into the realm of specific curricula. Where can character traits be incorporated into daily lessons? If we are talking about "honesty," how does it apply to math? Honesty safeguards the handling of people's money, for instance, from the simple act of making change to the full disclosure of risks in a particular investment. Where does it appear in science? Honesty insures the accuracy of experiments and test data. It dictates full disclosure of medical information to a patient. Where does honesty appear in the themes and characters of the literature we are studying? Where does it appear in social studies? In history? In art?

These questions are equally productive in individual settings as teachers adapt their lessons on an ongoing basis. Staff development in curriculum integration sharpens educators' ability to identify character education opportunities and equips them with techniques. They become adept at "seizing the moment," identifying situations that lend themselves to an exploration of a particular trait.

 ## Seizing the Moment

These moments occur dozens of times a day within the context of academic learning and social interactions. It takes training and a formalized intention to identify teachable moments and respond spontaneously. In an oxymoron, character education demands a "structured spontaneity." It is structured in the sense that the administration formally commits itself to an ongoing process and builds time into the system for it. "If the school board and the administration decide we're going to devote five minutes out of social studies or, more generally, ten minutes out of the day's collective instruction to character education, teachers can do it," explains Connie Lohse, an elementary school principal in the Mehlville district.

"But without such a mandate, character education gets lost in the time crunch."

Character education is not in danger of getting lost in the Brentwood District. It is kept in the forefront with a bull's-eye (Fogarty, 1991) rubber stamp and training that reinforces teachers' planning abilities. Each member of the faculty has a stamp and uses it to imprint the first page of each lesson plan. Concentric circles provide space to identify the critical-thinking skills and character traits related to the topic. For example, a math lesson on right triangles is stamped and completed as follows:

Bull's-Eye Planner

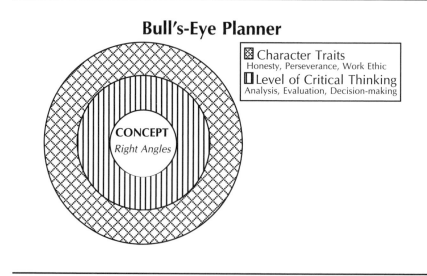

☒ Character Traits
Honesty, Perseverance, Work Ethic
☐ Level of Critical Thinking
Analysis, Evaluation, Decision-making

CONCEPT
Right Angles

This process connects the character trait to the concept with discussion questions: How do architects and builders use right angles in their design of homes, buildings and bridges? How important is the knowledge, precision and thoroughness of the architect and the builder? Give examples. What work ethics help architects and builders achieve optimum results and insure the safety of those who use their structures? Why is it important that these people have a high sense of character and that they care about the end result of their work (Archibald, 1995)?

The bull's-eye visually encourages teachers to create and incorporate character components within each lesson and, at the same time, provides immediate documentation of their work. It reflects a change in attitude that occurs as character education evolves.

"Instead of seeing it as a separate entity, a let's-stop-and-do-a-lesson-on-honesty approach, teachers begin to look at character education as a philosophy and a strategy for teaching," B. R. Rhoads says, recognizing the change in perception he has seen in his role as a national character education consultant.

Dee Blassie, a third grade teacher in the Parkway School District, finds the bull's-eye represents a synthesis of all she does in the classroom. She speaks of her "Dream Class," because her students come to believe that by setting goals and persevering, their dreams can come true. She blends content, learning strategies and instructional approaches in an environment permeated with character education.

The room is filled with positive messages and reinforcements. The words "empower" and "envision" float across the ceiling on paper clouds. The 15 traits her district emphasizes are posted on the walls. She examines one word a day, discussing such concepts as accountability, honesty, integrity, equality, and justice in terms her students can understand. The words are further illustrated in connection with class lessons and through cooperative learning experiences, chat times, community service projects and conflict-resolution training. She gives her students a high degree of responsibility: they help determine the rules of the classroom, check off their names when they turn in assignments, observe and compliment other students on good behavior, discuss their academic goals at the beginning of each quarter and formulate plans to achieve them, and build their own portfolios by filing the work they want to save throughout the year. Parents, welcome in her classroom at all times, are active partners in bringing dimension to the principles of character education.

Building a Lasting Infrastructure Within Schools and Districts

The process of integrating character education, whether into a classroom or throughout a district, takes years. An organizational structure that commits both personnel and time is essential. Superintendents of member districts appoint PREP coordinators at both the central office and building levels as they develop an infrastructure that builds character education into the system.

These coordinators, with written job responsibilities relating to character education, were initially funded by a U. S. Department of Education grant and are now supported by their respective districts. At the district level, coordinators design and facilitate staff development opportunities, initiate and coordinate system wide PREP activities, establish speakers' bureaus, locate community resources, and network. They often see their role as "planting seeds," suggesting ideas and resources rather than imposing expectations on individual schools.

Site coordinators, on the other hand, see that PREP is firmly rooted in the life of each school. Sensitive to the dynamics of the immediate community, they keep character education on the front burner, providing space and time for dialogue. They offer information and resources, encourage experimentation, coach individuals and teacher teams, network with representatives from other schools and districts, and plan staff development dedicated to character education skills and issues. Many develop PREP teams, involving other teachers, support staff and parents.

 ## Strengthening Character Education through Staff Development

Staff development, an integral component of PREP, reinforces skills that are closely allied with character education: cooperative learning, conflict resolution, authentic problem solving, self-assessment, service learning, computer technology, understanding of multiple intelligences, creation of caring classrooms, inclusion, multiculturalism, storytelling, whole language and integration across the curriculum. In addition, it places these skills in context as experts delineate the purpose of character education, its historical heritage, the pedagogy and the current efforts across the country.

National leaders such as Dr. Philip Vincent, author of *Developing Character in Students: A Primer for Teachers, Parents & Communities;* Dr. Thomas Lickona, author of *Educating for Character;* Dr. B. David Brooks, director of the Jefferson Center for Character Education and author of *A Case for Character Education*; Dr. Richard Kay, co-author of a guide to teaching respect, responsibility and excellence in the classroom; Mychal Wynn, author of *Empowering African-American Males to Succeed;* and Dr. Dorothy Rich, author of *MegaSkills,* have shared their philosophies with teachers and parents. They've presented lectures to large groups and worked more informally with small groups of teachers, basing their sessions on actual classroom experiences. Several staff development and training opportunities have included follow-up problem-solving and evaluation meetings for teachers implementing newly learned skills.

In addition, staff development is becoming more mobile and individualized as it responds to the needs of schools. CSD is developing a cadre of teachers trained in character education who work on-site with school staffs. "Train the Trainer" sessions target teachers who are experienced in a combination of strategies and innovations. These teachers receive an in-depth grounding in the pedagogy and process of character education.

Coordinating a Metropolitan-Wide Effort

PREP is based on the premise of an active partnership between school, home and community. It has developed a structure from these components that works on a small scale—within a classroom, school or single district, as well as on the broader landscape of a metropolitan area.

Three advisory councils channel the energies of business and community leaders, superintendents, administrators, teachers, support staff and parents toward the goals of character education.

The first, a 26-member Planning and Advisory Committee, involves representatives from businesses and corporations, foundations, youth organizations, law enforcement, the media, education, parents and community agencies. This group provides overall direction, raises funds and marshals essential community resources. In the St. Louis area, more than 40 companies, foundations and individuals have contributed to PREP, including Monsanto, McDonnell Douglas, the Danforth Foundation, Emerson Electric, Southwestern Bell, Anheuser Busch and other local companies.

Industry specialists have advised educators in the development of courses. Businesses have contributed printing, lent staff to public relations efforts and offered other in-kind contributions; local storefronts have posted their district's character traits; a television station has produced a weekly Saturday morning storytelling program focused on character traits. More recently, the *St. Louis Post-Dispatch* initiated a nine-part series, exploring particular traits through the lives of individual students and the people and programs that influenced them. The CBS affiliate airs brief "Word of the Month" features during family programming. The city and county police departments joined CSD efforts, sponsoring "Do the Right Thing." This ongoing program honors several students each month for acts of character and is supported by coverage in the daily newspaper and both the CBS and NBC affiliates.

The support of major employers in the area is often critical in getting started and, as more than one superintendent has observed, the key to sustaining the program. They offer potential fundraising support but, even more important, they employ parents whose students attend the schools. Their involvement completes the circle, reinforcing the significance of character education for the entire community.

The second council, the Superintendents Committee, is charged with expansion and financial management decisions. The actual superintendents (no substitutes) convene three times a year to review fiscal policy, share their district's progress, and develop collaborative efforts. Together, they produced a checklist of what superintendents can do in support of character education. This aspect of the PREP model is easily fulfilled by administrators or the principal of a school when character education involves a single district or school.

The third body, the Development Team, comprises educators from all participating districts—principals, counselors, teachers and assistant superintendents. This team is the engine of the project, propelling character education within the schools and throughout the metropolitan community, defining staff development based on the needs of their constituents, and setting the course for the future. The team approves projects, qualifying them for matching fund support, and pools the ideas that result, sharing them with other districts. This component, on a smaller scale, invites the creation of teams involving parents, teachers and administrators who facilitate character education initiatives in the classroom.

In addition to the councils, the administrative center of PREP is within an organization that has a 65-year legacy of collaboration among the St. Louis metropolitan area districts. Cooperating Schools Districts provide the depth of resources in staff development, technology, public relations, and access to administrators, educators parents, and community leaders that secures PREP. PREP, in turn, provides the continuity of support that fortifies the work of character education in the districts and the schools.

Evaluating the Impact of PREP

Evaluation, a critical factor in PREP's success, continues on both an ongoing and annual basis. Surveys, debriefing sessions after major programs and conferences, focus groups and dialogue sessions provide immediate feedback. A comprehensive study conducted each year by an outside consultant includes several components: site observations and interviews, surveys of teachers and students and internal studies by districts. The impartial review targets three questions: Has PREP become part of the permanent structure of the schools? Has character education curricula been implemented effectively in participating schools? What student outcomes have resulted?

The findings have supported the thrust of PREP and its efforts to integrate character education into the existing curricula and the life of the schools. Feedback has helped to fine-tune administrative capabilities and illuminate areas of weakness. One recurring find, for instance, is that PREP is teacher-dependent. "It will always be teacher-dependent," McKay says. "As a result, staff development and support will always be essential to the success of the program."

While data gathering and analysis provide answers to the first two questions, the third, student outcomes, is more difficult to quantify. "We've tried various ways to determine if children are more honest, responsible and cooperative as a result of PREP," explains Dr. Michael P. Grady, a St. Louis University professor of education and the consultant who designed the evaluation process. The responses of more than 10,000 students to the 1995 survey show general agreement that an emphasis on personal responsibility has improved behavior, that the school cares about them, and that they recognize their responsibility to assist other students. Yet these responses do not measure actual change. Grady hopes to record quantifiable data with an in-depth longitudinal study beginning in 1996. He will limit the study to three districts and intensify the focus on outcomes.

While Grady continues his research, people in the field offer individual feedback on outcomes. For instance, Juanita Doggett, principal of Sherman Elementary Community Education Center in St. Louis, notes improved conduct (only three referrals for bus misconduct in the previous year), an average 94 percent student-attendance rate and rising academic achievement scores. "We work hard at joining hands with our parents and our community to stress good citizenship. I firmly believe that a focus like this impacts children's behavior, helps their self-esteem and motivates them to learn," says Doggett.

Two second grade teachers from the Parkway district in St. Louis county reported fewer behavior problems in their classrooms after the Jefferson Center's "Responsibility Skills" program was introduced. "Despite our fears that this was going to take time away from instruction, it actually saved time," they said.

Jo Ann Jasin, principal of Wedgwood Elementary School, notes that the concepts are commingled into everything from the cafeteria line to the playground to the science class. Her school was one of the first St. Louis area schools to implement a comprehensive character education program in 1989. The number of referrals to the principal's office decreased 24 percent in the first three years. The number of students reading at or above the national average rose from 65 to 70 percent in that time.

Student comments reflect the influence of character education, from the fifth grader who said, "I used to have trouble in math and my friends made fun of me. Now my friends help me," to a high school freshman who reflected: "It's given me a better way to think through my choices. If something is wrong, I know why it's wrong."

Where We Are Within the Schools

Newcomers to PREP discover a wealth of resources for each phase of the process: reaching consensus on a list of traits, creating a comfort level, and integrating character education into the academic and social life of the schools. Newcomers add breadth to PREP, while veteran districts weave character education into more and more aspects of school life.

Character education has become entrenched in elementary schools over the past eight years and has found secure footing in advisories or special periods at the middle school level, but it is just beginning to take hold at the secondary level. The strides some high school teachers are making show the diversity and creativity of their efforts, e.g., a student-run credit union founded on business ethics, computer training based on moral issues in the work world, a student initiative that resulted in an off-campus conference on character issues, an English literature class with a rigorous reading schedule based on such themes as "How do we make moral choices?" and "finding purpose in our lives," and an ambitious service-learning curriculum.

Service learning is far from confined to the secondary level. It provides such immediate opportunities to express the traits and internalize them that interest at all grade levels has intensified. Schools are developing both optional and mandatory courses and strengthening their extracurricular programs with student-directed research and planning; training in problem-solving, empathic listening, communication, decision-making and helping skills; education in the traditions of philanthropy, citizenship and activism; and reflection and evaluation of their experiences. PREP's annual symposium doubled its previous attendance figures in 1995, attracting more than 400 teachers, students and parents.

 ## Moving Toward Self-Sufficiency

Staffs from more than half of the 30 PREP districts are engaged in curriculum integration. At the same time, all of the districts are assuming an increasing proportion of PREP costs as they move the organization toward the goal of financial self-sufficiency. Substantial contributions from corporations and foundations during the formative years of the project were recognized as essential start-up support, but not as a continuing resource. With an accelerated schedule of annual dues, the districts will provide more than half of the metropolitan-wide administrative costs of PREP by 1997, as well as supporting their own character education programs.

 ## Moving Into the Future

The direction of the future is twofold. PREP is reaching upward to university education departments, examining ways to offer both the pedagogy and the skills of character education to prospective teachers. PREP is also reaching inward. Its penetration within the 393 member schools is far from even. In some schools, particularly at the elementary level, character education permeates the physical and academic structure. It's become a way of life. In others, it is confined to an individual or small group of teachers, or relegated to the departments of counseling, health or consumer science. The goal is to increase the influence and effectiveness of these forces until character education is present in every classroom.

A Universal Process

Two years ago we changed the name of Personal Responsibility Education Process (PREP), substituting "Process" where "Program" once appeared. In a world of acronyms, the change was so subtle it called little attention to itself, but it expressed what we realized in retrospect. The structures of PREP, the elements that give it form and substance, serve or facilitate the underlying processes. The liveliness of the organization springs not so much from "what it is" but "how it does what it does." These patterns of action are universal. While the St. Louis metropolitan structure of PREP may be difficult for other communities to replicate, the processes—strategies for achieving consensus within a community, a comfort level within the schools, grass-roots innovation and ongoing curriculum modification—adapt easily to other settings. We've seen it work. Communities, districts and individual schools, both public and private, throughout this country and others, have used PREP as a model in the development of their character education initiatives.

References

Archibald, G., Berg, S., Stirling D., McKay, L. *How to PREP: Using Character Education in Schools, Homes and the Community.* St. Louis, Missouri: Personal Responsibility Education Process, Cooperating School Districts, 1995.

Brooks, B. David. *Responsibility Skills: "Lessons for Success," Elementary School Curriculum.* Pasadena, CA: Jefferson Center for Character Education, 1990.

Brooks, B. David. *The Case for Character Education.* Ottawa, IL: Green Hill Publishers, 1983. Revised edition to be released in spring of 1996.

Fogarty, R. *The Mindful School: How to Integrate the Curriculum.* Palatine, IL: IRI Skylight Publishing, Inc., 1991.

Kay, R. S. and Kay, D. S. *The Best Is Within Us. Propositions, principles and strategies for teaching respect, responsibility, and excellence in the classroom.* Salt Lake City, UT, 1994.

Lickona, T. *Educating for Character: How Our Schools Can Teach Respect and Responsibility.* New York: Bantam Books, 1991.

Lions-Quest *Skills for Growing.* Granville, OH: Quest International, 1990.

Lions-Quest *Skills for Adolescence.* Granville, OH: Quest International, 1992.

Lions-Quest *Skills for Action.* Granville, OH: Quest International, 1995.

McKay, L. (Ed.) "PREP Words and Definitions." St. Louis, MO: Personal Responsibility Education Process, Cooperating School Districts, 1994

"Superintendents Checklist for Character Education." St. Louis, MO: Personal Responsibility Education Process, Cooperating School Districts, 1994.

Rich, D. *MegaSkills: How Families Can Help Children Succeed in School and Beyond.* Boston, MA: Houghton Mifflin, 1988.

Wynn, M. *Empowering African-American Males to Succeed.* South Pasadena, CA: Rising Sun Publications, 1992.

Background Information

Personal Responsibility Education Process (PREP), a project of the Cooperating School Districts (CSD)–13157 Olive Spur Rd., St. Louis, Missouri, 63141. (314) 576-3535, ext. 130. Fax: (314) 576-4996.

Principal Staff Members:

Linda McKay, with an extensive background in community leadership, has served as director of the Cooperating School Districts' Personal Responsibility Education Process (PREP) since 1989, one year after its formation.

Dr. Jerry Corley, with 31 years in public school administration, teaching and coaching, facilitates and supports the process of curriculum integration in PREP member districts. He is the PREP curriculum integration coordinator for Cooperating School Districts.

Copy for this chapter was prepared by Diane Stirling, a freelance writer who works closely with PREP. Contact information: phone (314) 965-5423; fax (314) 965-5423

3 AMHERST, NY

A K-12 Success Story in Values Education Increases Awareness in Values Practices in New York's Sweet Home Community

Sharon L. Banas

THE GOAL OF THE "Foundations for Our Future: Values, Youth and Our Schools" New York State Department of Education's Conference in 1988 was to make educators aware of the need for values education as an integral element for students' success. The conference's focus was on encouraging school districts to develop comprehensive programs in this vein. New York State's *Compact for Learning* states that "when the school reflects the values of the home and the home supports the efforts of the school, children grow in an atmosphere of shared purpose and consistent expectations."

The Sweet Home Central School District, located in the towns of Amherst and Tonawanda, a suburb of Buffalo, NY, accepted the challenge. In keeping with the African proverb, "It takes a whole village to raise a child," Sweet Home involved its whole district in developing a values education program that would truly reflect the needs of the community.

The Sweet Home community is composed of middle-income residents mirroring many typical communities throughout New York State. The State University of New York at Buffalo is its neighbor, and a large industrial park is located within the district. There are six schools: four elementary (K-5), one middle school (6-8), and one high school (9-12). The total student population is approximately 4,000. Peak enrollment occurred in the 1973-74 school year when there were 7,524 students. Two elementary schools were closed in 1981 and 1988. It is a culturally diverse area and has seen an increasing number of students who do not have English as their primary language.

Dr. James N. Finch, superintendent of schools, sent Sharon Banas, a middle-school social studies teacher to the 1988 department of education conference. In the fall he sent out a memorandum to all staff members stating that the district was interested in undertaking a comprehensive values- education program, and invited interested individuals to respond. The responses clearly indicated tremendous support for the idea. In his initial letter Dr. Finch stated, "...building values in children is an important task that has to be shared by parents, school personnel and community groups. In school, the role of support personnel is of critical importance in teaching children how to behave, how to treat one another and to understand their obligations. The school bus, lunchrooms and corridors are ideal places to teach important values."

In November, 1988, a District Values Education Council was formed to be chaired by Sharon Banas. The 24-member group include representation from all six buildings, administrators, teachers, parents, a member of the board of education, bus drivers, director of athletics, and other support staff.

The district invited Dr. Thomas Lickona, author of *Raising Good Children* (1983) and *Educating for Character* (1991), to come to Sweet Home in February, 1989, to conduct a series of workshops for the entire community. The first jobs of the Values Education Council were to plan the workshops with Dr. Lickona, review the mission and goal statement, and establish a district philosophy. The philosophy is "to develop *climates* or *atmospheres* in our buildings that foster the development of good values for our children, and to assist them in using these values to make better decisions in their lives."

With the support of the board of education, values education was adopted as a top district priority in the 1989-90 and 1990-91 school years. Study plans were developed and implemented throughout the district.

Mini-grants were made available for supplementary funds through the curriculum office. Since values education was a district priority, teachers, administrators, bus drivers, librarians, etc. wrote for these grants to receive financial assistance for various values projects.

A decision was also made that every building program would be unique to that building, and today the buildings claim proud ownership of these programs. Each building also formed a values committee that included parents and students, as well as a diverse representation of individuals who deal with their children every day. However, even though the building programs were to be unique, the Council agreed that values education throughout the district would contain five key elements.

First, values education would be a comprehensive, systematic, planned K-12 program involving district, building and classroom activities. William Kilpatrick, in his book *Why Johnny Can't Tell Right From Wrong* (1992), states, "The primary way to bring ethics and character back into the schools is to create a positive moral environment in schools. The ethos of the school, not its course offerings, is the decisive factor in forming good character."

Second, it is an infused, integrated approach. Sweet Home would not write a curriculum or buy a packaged product, but would use their own personnel as the experts. The Council never wanted values education to be thought of as an "add-on." Sharon Banas, the Values Education Coordinator for the district, states that, "This decision has also kept the program alive, growing and exciting, because the committees are constantly adding and adapting ideas to the district, building and classroom activities." It has also given the district a sense of true ownership of the program.

Third, it is a very visible program. One cannot enter a Sweet Home school without an immediate awareness of the involvement in teaching good values. For example, in Sweet Home middle Sschool there are large, colorful vinyl banners that state: "I Am Responsible For My Day," "I Want Respect And I Show It," or "I Respect Others, Myself, and My School." In the cafeteria there is a banner that states, "Courtesy is Contagious." At Willow Ridge Elementary, people walk down a *Hall Of Values,* where ten beautifully framed posters depict the values in their value-a-month program.

Fourth, it is a language-based program. Children need to be taught the meaning of values such as respect, responsibility, trustworthiness, etc. In Sweet Home's newly revised *Values Education Handbook*, activities are organized under values that are clearly defined with examples of how to practice them. An awareness is also needed so that everyone constantly uses the terminology and reinforces the values.

Last, the program should be well advertised throughout the community. A description about the Council is added to the district calendar, school handbooks have been revised, articles are written in all school papers and the PTA's report on activities at all meetings, etc. Ms. Banas says, "When you involve your entire community and keep them well informed, you eliminate the controversy, because these are values everyone agrees upon for our society. Parents have never told us that they didn't want us to teach their children to show respect for themselves and others, or be more responsible."

One of the first decisions to be made by the building committees was which values to emphasize in their building. At Sweet Home Middle School, a values committee decided to concentrate on Respect and Responsibility because these seemed to be the most important at this level, and because many values seemed to fall under these two headings, as Dr. Lickona had illustrated in his workshops. At that time the committee developed a sheet on Respect and another on Responsibility, listing examples of how individuals exhibit these values. These were printed on card stock paper in school colors and posted in every room in the middle school.

At Willow Ridge Elementary, the values committee decided to survey the parents on the back of the school menu. They listed 20 of the commonly agreed upon values and asked the parents to choose the ones they felt should be emphasized in their school. Using the results of the survey, they began their successful value-a-month program. The top three choices of the community were self-worth, respect and responsibility.

People often ask how this program spread to involve the cafeterias, offices and school buses. Basically, it was because people in charge of these services were part of the district and building committees from the very onset of the program. In the middle school, for example, Jack Ault, the head custodian, decided that the school cafeteria needed a more positive environment. He recognized that displaying the artistic talents of many of the students was a way to do this. The PTA provided the funds for large snap-open frames, and Mr. Ault got the art department to supply the students' art work to display in the frames. Now the cafeteria looks like an art gallery, and the custodians change the selections regularly to give other students the opportunity to see their work on display. The cafeteria also functions as an auditorium for community events, so parents often admire the work of the students as well.

The bus drivers were also led by a few key individuals who formed a district committee. They sent out a letter asking other drivers to assist them in their efforts. They posted signs on all of the buses stating that these are "positive buses." Several of the drivers went for training and are teaching a bus-safety program in primary classrooms, emphasizing the importance of good behavior and respect for each other and property.

The bus drivers' values committee also adopted an idea from Mary Zimmerman, a driver and chairperson on their values committee. A "Caring Day" was organized throughout the district on which all of the elementary and middle school students were given a piece of green ribbon. Each driver explained that the color green represents *growing* and *caring* and since caring was a value they were working on in school, they should give the ribbon to an adult in the building who showed care and concern for them. Some drivers were stationed at the doors of each building to give ribbons to those students who had not ridden a school bus that day. Students gave ribbons to secretaries, cafeteria workers, guidance counselors and teachers who wore them proudly.

A major part of the values program has been the recognition of the importance of people like the bus drivers. Many wonderful things began to happen when the teachers and administrators asked for their input and acknowledged the importance of their role with the students. The bus drivers' values committee asked for and received training workshops and speakers for the drivers.

Some of the drivers also began to attend staff-development workshops targeted for teachers. Their photos were included in the yearbooks, as well as the photos of secretaries, custodians and cafeteria workers. Principals hosted receptions for them to discuss common concerns and expectations, and students began asking them to attend after school events. A parent, Sandy Radens, submitted an editorial to the local newspaper expressing her appreciation for the drivers' professionalism and the kindliness they offered her children, especially in stressful situations. Some of the bus drivers have chaperoned middle school activity nights, and they sponsored a poster contest on good bus behavior. They contacted local businesses for prizes and actually gave away two ten-speed bicycles to the top winners.

The Sweet Home Teacher Center has been important in providing books, materials and in-service workshops on values-related issues. The librarians developed values bibliographies of books contained in each school library that are categorized by grade level and the values being emphasized in that building. This is a wonderful resource for teachers who can simply check the list when they are in need of some literature to promote a certain value in their lessons.

Parents have been involved from the very beginning as active participants on the district and building committees. They report regularly at their meetings. At one of the final meetings of the district PTA Council, each president is asked to summarize the major values activities conducted in their building during the past school year. Many parent workshops have also been conducted throughout the district where parents can share common concerns. Ms. Banas meets with the parents who serve on the building committees once a year to get their input as the district Values Education Council establishes goals for the coming school year.

There has been no parental objection to this program in Sweet Home, but rather, it has been supported and encouraged by parents. Dee Serrio, a parent and former president of the District PTA Council, says, "The Values Education program just gives us more leverage at home because parents are working with our schools to teach values agreed upon by all of us." The high school PTSA decided that, when they chose the high school seniors who would receive their scholarships, they would not use the standard essay question about why the student feels they deserve the scholarship, but would instead pose an ethical question. Values issues have become that important in our district. The first question developed by the parents was:

> Everyone in your Introduction to Psychology Course is cheating on exams. Your professor is aware but unconcerned. You can't bring yourself to cheat, but are failing due to the curve. How do you survive this required course? (Justify your answer in 75-150 words).

The values-education program in the Sweet Home Central School District actually functions at three levels: district/community, building and classroom. The ultimate assistance offered to families occurs through the Family Support Center which serves as a true partnership between the family, the school and the community. It was initiated by the district and organized by a variety of social service agencies. The Center serves as a link to community-based human services in a convenient school setting.

The Family Support Center focuses on supporting families' social, educational and physical needs. The Center works toward strengthening families so that their children can become productive adults. The Center works with agencies to provide advocacy, assessment, prevention and intervention support for parents and students. The school district hired a full-time coordinator for the center, Kim Cassidy, and through grant monies, secured a parent involvement specialist, Mary Rose. The Center has been so successful in the past two years that the United Way has contributed a $25,000 grant each year, enabling the Center to continue to assist families.

We do not live in an ideal world, and the administration in Sweet Home District believe that when community problems arise they need to be addressed openly. For example, in February, 1994, the superintendent of schools, Dr. Gary Cooper, sent a very frank letter to parents stating, "Many of our young people are using and/or abusing alcohol and other substances, creating problems in school." He went on to ask parents to join together at a town meeting at Sweet Home High School because "as a community we need to pool our resources and talents in order to work together, not only to protect our children from substance abuse, but to protect them from the serious human tragedies which follow increases in drug and alcohol usage." On a snowy evening, over 200 parents joined together with local agencies to discuss these issues at the town meeting. Subsequent meetings and workshops have continued as a result of the concerns and strategies discussed at that meeting.

At the district level, the Values Education Council and the Drug/Substance Abuse Council worked jointly in sponsoring evening forums for parents and students. Average attendance at the two forums that have been conducted so far is over 800 students and parents.

At the building level there may be special projects, displays, assemblies, themes, etc. For example, at Glendale Elementary, the most diverse of the district's elementary schools, one of the highlights of the year is the "Celebration of Unity Week," started by the building values committee. This week-long event was designed to celebrate the cultural diversity of the school community and create an atmosphere of mutual understanding for all cultures and beliefs. The students research other countries. Each child makes a flag representing their nationality and they are used to decorate the halls.

An Information Day is held when Sweet Home High School students and community members visit Glendale and present programs about various cultures. Students attend cooking demonstrations. Each student is given a passport to complete their own personal information. As they "travel" to other countries (through presentations) on Information Day their passports are stamped so they have a record of the countries they learned about that day. In math class, they calculate the distance they traveled that day. Morning assembly programs are held in which different classes prepare performances. Students put on short plays, sing, read poetry or perform ethnic dances. Parents participate by supplying artifacts and displays that describe the country of their origin. These artifacts are on display in the building all week. Parents and teachers supply traditional foods for a "Taste of Nations" evening for the community. Attendance at this event has been overwhelming!

At Maplemere Elementary, a building project that received a great deal of attention was the creation of *A Big Book of Good Judgment.* Every K-5 child had a page illustrated and laminated in this book. In the 1994-95 school year, Maplemere chose as their values theme for the year "In the Year of the Peaceful Solution," and concentrated the entire year on conflict resolution training for all teachers and students. Fourth and fifth grade students who want to serve as values leaders on the building committee must apply and then attend training workshops usually held on parent-teacher conference days when the students would normally not be in attendance.

At Sweet Home Middle School there have also been many building projects. They have a "Caring Calendar" that contains a daily message, selected by the students, which is read each morning at the end of announcements, and flashed on the electronic message board provided by the PTA for the cafeteria. One of the current building projects involves the selection of "People of Character." The goal of the activity is the recognition of positive role models among us. A sheet listing the qualities of "A Person of Character" was received from the Josephson School of Ethics in California in conjunction with the National Character Counts Week designated by Congress in 1994. This was distributed to all of the teachers. The school handed out pencils printed with "Character Counts at Sweet Home Middle."

The values committee sponsors a T-shirt contest and a special T-shirt is designed by the winning students. Nomination forms are available in the school office and enclosed in the community newsletter. A committee of four teachers, two parents, four students and a staff member meet to review the nominations and honor the recipients. Teachers, parents, non-teaching staff, students, and administrators have all been nominated for the award.

The values committee has also sponsored special activities to make the celebration of holidays more meaningful to the students. In November, every student was given an interview form and a social studies assignment to interview a veteran before Veterans' Day. If a student did not know a veteran, there were bus drivers, administrators, teachers and custodians who agreed to be interviewed by the students. The impact of these interviews was tremendous. Students carried to school memorabilia given to them by veterans of all conflicts, including World War I. Some sixth grade classes wrote letters to veterans in the local hospital and received wonderful responses. Others journeyed to the hospital and performed in a talent show for the veterans. Students also made a beautiful banner thanking our veterans that now hangs in the dining hall at the hospital.

The values program is enhanced through wonderful classroom programs and activities. An outstanding example was a classroom project designed by Mark Basehart for his fifth graders at Heritage Heights Elementary. The project was called "Home Is Where the Heart Is." It was a Dimensions of Learning unit developed by focusing on the concept of home. The unit incorporated activities crossing the spectrum of multiple intelligences empowering students to think creatively and critically about various levels of "home"—a house, a special place, a community, the earth—while exploring the social issue of homelessness. A linkage was made with a fourth grade class from School #67 in the City of Buffalo. Over 100 students from both schools actually participated in the project.

Students volunteered at Friends of the Night soup kitchen, engaged in reading quality literature focusing on issues of home/homelessness and reflected on their experiences in their writer's notebooks. The students' entries were then collected into an anthology being sold by the PTA with all proceeds benefiting the Friends of the Night people.

Margery Baumler, member of the Board of Education and the District Values Council, says, "The development of this comprehensive, planned program in Sweet Home has simply given credibility to our teachers and approval for teaching these values overtly." Teachers have always viewed their profession as a moral one, and most entered teaching to make a difference in the lives of children. Now they have the support they need to bring forth ideas, activities and strategies they have always believed were for the benefit of their students.

In Sweet Home, teachers discovered they did not need a curriculum, because they were eager to support the values program in their classrooms. A great deal can be done to support values learning through the use of literature. Some teachers have adopted a practice of placing a weekly quote or a simple thought at the bottom of dittos given out to students. Likewise, social studies teachers use historical documents. The social studies department at the high school has received several human relations awards. The New York State curriculum for the ninth and tenth grades is "Global Studies." After the students complete the study of one area/people of the world, the social studies teachers immerse them in that culture for a day.

The home and careers department at the middle school decided to expand the required component on decision-making skills in seventh grade. They discuss the importance of using good values to make decisions, and in eighth grade discuss ethics in the world of work as each class does an entrepreneurship. The health department emphasizes respect for our bodies. The science department involves students in extensive projects demonstrating respect for the environment. Values can be taught deliberately every day in every classroom. If teachers cannot think of a way to connect it to the content, they can do so by reinforcing classroom rules or by bringing it out in a strategy like cooperative learning.

How does the district measure the effectiveness of this program? The very nature of the program makes it difficult to measure. The district has administered surveys to staff, parents and students. One of the elementary buildings conducts a staff survey after every major building project.

Some national groups feel that attendance records, number of discipline referrals and student grades can be used, but these may not be true indicators because of all the variables that can cause these results. However, at Sweet Home Middle School there have recently been marking periods where 60% of the students were on the merit or honor roll and almost 50% had perfect attendance. At the high school, the values committee began a project called STARS (Students That Are Really Special). The purpose of the program is to recognize good students who do their best but may not be honor roll students or great athletes. In order for a student to be a STAR the criteria are: an average of 80 or higher, only one absence during the marking period, no late arrivals to school, and no referrals to the administration for behavior problems. A breakfast is prepared by parents and teachers, a former graduate of Sweet Home delivers an inspirational message and students are awarded certificates and ribbons. The number of students eligible and attending these breakfasts has more than doubled since the first one.

There has also been a real consciousness of community and world problems that is not always a part of the school syllabus. Elementary students have raised money for victims of the Oklahoma bombing, as well as for hurricane, earthquake and flood victims. There have been values activities to reach out to grandparents, senior citizens and families in need in our own community. Middle school students have assisted families with mentally ill children, collected toys for a needy day care center and hired themselves out to do jobs, raising enough money to have a room dedicated to them at a drug treatment center for adolescents. High school students have answered elementary students' letters to Santa Claus, tutored middle schoolers, volunteered at shelters for the homeless and run bloodmobiles for the American Red Cross.

As coordinator of the project, Ms. Banas states that one of the greatest measurements of effectiveness for her has been conversations with administrators, teachers, staff and students who say that the values program has given them a keener awareness about the importance of their job as role models for others. She says, "Perhaps in the process of trying to raise better students at Sweet Home, we are also creating better teachers, administrators, etc."

The Sweet Home Values Education Program continues to grow and remain as exciting as it was in the 1989-90 school year when it began. The support of central office and the board of education has been critical and accounts for the fact that this is truly a community project and involves all six buildings. The Sweet Home Board of Education has drafted unanimous resolutions showing continuous support and agreement that their schools will work toward "...assisting youth in the development of civic virtue and moral character for a more compassionate and responsible society," as stated in the mission statement of the National Character Education Partnership.

The Sweet Home Central School District has a clear vision, stated in its strategic plan and new mission statement, that continues to guide the district. The mission statement reads as follows:

To develop lifelong learners prepared for the challenges of their future, the Sweet Home district will empower all students to think both creatively and critically while becoming cooperative, self-directed citizens through active learning experiences where educators, in partnership with the community, serve as resources and guides in the pursuit of student excellence.

References

Kilpatrick, William. *Why Johnny Can't Tell Right From Wrong.* New York: Simon and Schuster, 1992.

Likona, Thomas. *Raising Good Children.* New York: Bantam Books, 1983.

_____. *Educating For Character: How Our Nation's Schools Can Teach Respect and Responsibility.* New York: Bantam Books, 1991.

Sweet Home School District's *Values Education Handbook.* Community Education Office, 1901 Sweet Home Road, Amherst, NY 14228. Phone: (716) 689-5215.

The Character Education Partnership. 1250 N. Pitt Street, Alexandria, VA 22314. Phone: (703) 739-9515 or (800) 988-8081; fax: (703) 549-3891.

The Michael and Edna Josephson Institute for Ethics. 310 Washington Blvd., Suite 104, Marina del Ray, CA 90292. Phone: (310) 827-1864; fax: (703) 549-3891.

Celebrating Character
in Cumberland County Schools
Engenders Positive Community Support

Carol Leslie–Hudson

Director, Drug Awareness Programs

CITIZENS OF CUMBERLAND COUNTY are coming together to "Celebrate Character." Thousands of people have participated in summits to develop strategies to promote character. The local school system has encouraged religious leaders, elected officials, parents, law enforcement officers, military corps, media personalities, youth organizations and others to join in a unified campaign. This initiative began as a response to serious problems facing the community.

Introduction

Located in eastern North Carolina, Cumberland County is the home of Fort Bragg, the largest military reservation in the United States, and Pope Air Force Base, one of the oldest installations of the Air Force. The area boasts the highest concentration of retail sales dollars spent in the state while at the same time is urban, suburban and rural. The total population of approximately 276,500 is the most multicultural in the state.

Fayetteville State University (FSU) is the fastest-growing institution of higher education in the state and has the distinction of being the first state-supported normal school for Black Americans in the South. Fayetteville is also home to Methodist College, a four-year liberal arts and sciences college.

Cumberland County Schools is the fourth-largest school system in North Carolina and the 75th-largest system in the United States. The student population is approximately 51,000 and is increasing an average of 1,200 students a year. The system's 72 schools include 50 elementary schools, 12 middle schools, eight high schools, an alternative secondary school and a special school for exceptional children. It is the largest school system in the state designated as a low-wealth system. In 1993-94, it ranked 110th of 121 school systems in per pupil expenditure and 120th in funding in the state. Furthermore, overcrowding is a serious problem. Poverty and lack of space contribute to tension and discord.

As is true across the nation, Cumberland County is experiencing the impact of crime, drugs and violence rampant in our society. Recently, Morgan Quitmo Press, a Kansas publisher, described Fayetteville as the ninth most dangerous place to live in the country. Cumberland County's youths are especially endangered. They are victims as well as the perpetrators of violent crimes, giving the county the second-worst violent youth crime rate in North Carolina.

School Superintendent John R. Griffin, Jr. decided to take action by posing the question to the community "Should the schools teach character?" In order to answer his question, representatives from the schools held a Character Education Summit in February, 1994. A delegation of community leaders, including parents, business persons, religious leaders and school personnel, were recruited from each school to attend the summit. Despite torrential rain on the evening of the summit, over 500 citizens came out to talk about character education in the schools.

Creating Consensus

After the opening comments, the summit delegates participated in a small group consensus-building process. There was immediate consensus that the schools needed to become more actively involved in moral education. Then the participants identified the virtues they wanted addressed. Afterwards, the small groups joined with one another and continued the lively discussion, while group facilitators assured that every person contributed. At the end of the summit, group facilitators turned in a summary of their group's consensus. Interested participants signed up to serve on a task force to further design the program.

The next month, the schools held a youth summit for character education. The 20 middle and high schools sent delegations of young people who participated in the same type of consensus-building process. These students were representative of their overall student populations in terms of race, sex and academic achievement. It was noteworthy that the top three concepts identified by adults and youth were the same: respect, responsibility and integrity.

Developing a Plan

The Character Education Task Force began meeting in April, 1994. The first items of business were to compile the results of the summits and to develop a mission statement. The superintendent selected a member of the central office staff of the schools to coordinate the initiative.

The five character traits determined to be priorities from the two summits were:

Respect
Responsibility
Integrity
Caring
Self-Discipline

Although there are other important values, such as honesty and courage, the group agreed these are components of the stated five. Some time later, the task force became aware of the national Character Counts! Coalition and their six pillars of character. It surprised members of the task force to learn that Dr. Lloyd V. Hackley, then Chancellor of Fayetteville State University, is a member of the Character Counts! Council of Advisers and Advocates. Dr. Hackley came and spoke with the task force to encourage them to align themselves with the six pillars of character as described by the Coalition. These are:

Trustworthiness
Respect
Responsibility
Fairness
Caring
Citizenship

Obviously, the list generated locally and the Character Counts! pillars were very similar. The task force was reluctant to abandon the work of the community while at the same time it wanted to be a part of this national force in character education development. The task force members decided to add those "pillars" that were not already a part of the local list, bringing the number of concepts to eight. A similar process was used to come to consensus on the definitions to be used.

 ## Concepts Of Character

1. **Respect**: To act with courtesy, tolerance and dignity.
2. **Responsibility**: To be dependable and accountable for one's actions.
3. **Integrity**: To have the inner strength to adhere to high ethical standards.
4. **Caring**: To demonstrate kindness, consideration & compassion.
5. **Self-Discipline**: To exercise positive self-control.
6. **Trustworthiness**: To be worthy of confidence.
7. **Fairness**: To be impartial and equitable.
8. **Citizenship**: To honor and contribute to the laws, policies and human rights of the land.

After considerable discussion, the task force wrote a mission statement as follows:

> Cumberland County Schools acknowledges that its role is to reinforce traditional values and positive character that originate and are fostered in the home.
>
> We will, through collaborative community efforts, teach and model fundamentals of good character to include respect, responsibility and integrity to all students.

The task force reviewed the research and literature on character education, existing programs currently being used in the schools, and other available programs in order to make recommendations for implementation. The task force formed a research committee to review the literature and present its findings to the task force. This provided members with an overview and a common frame of reference.

Next, the task force invited curriculum specialists to identify and discuss curricula currently being implemented across the county. The task force recognized that many programs already had a strong basis in character development and would provide a strong foundation for the initiative. Representatives who market other programs in support of character education curricula were invited to share their ideas. Spokespersons from across the nation presented information to the task force. After much discussion and review, the task force decided to refer curriculum selection to a committee of educators. This committee would be responsible for coming back to the task force with recommendations.

The task force then went on to identify key principles for implementing effective character education. Using the six principles established by Kenneth Burrett and Timothy Rusnak (1993) as a guideline, the task force decided:

- Character education must be well supported by research and tailored to the needs of the community.
- Character education must be an integral part of the curriculum.
- Character education must be offered from kindergarten through the twelfth grades.
- Home, school and community are vital collaborative partners in the character education of young people.
- In order to effectively teach character education, one must model the fundamentals of good character to include respect, responsibility and integrity.
- Staff development and parent involvement are critical in implementing a successful character education program.
- Peers can be used effectively in teaching and modeling character traits.
- A positive school climate fosters character development.
- Consequences for non-compliance must be firmly established and adhered to, assuring respect, responsibility and integrity.

The local board of education approved these principles. These guidelines provided a framework or guiding philosophy, out of which the program grew. The task force continued to meet to provide oversight and guidance for the initiative. At the same time, three committees carried on the work of preparing for implementation.

Integrating the Curriculum

The curriculum-review committee was established to recommend strategies for implementation and integration. Members of the committee included teachers at the elementary, middle and high school levels, guidance counselors, exceptional children's teachers, and curriculum specialists. The committee immediately agreed that the best approach would be through integration into the existing curriculum, as opposed to acquiring a new program.

Since the state of North Carolina has a standard course of study, this was the obvious place to start. Although character education crosses all curriculum areas, those that most easily lend themselves to character development are social studies, English and literature, guidance and counseling, and healthful living. The committee reviewed the competency goals and objectives for each subject area and noted those related to the specific character concepts. This allowed for correlation with the state curriculum, the local order of instruction, and the character concept of the month.

A reading list by grade levels and character concepts is used to supplement the English curriculum. The Workforce Development teachers developed a number of integrated lessons related to career development and correlated the character concepts. The Drug Abuse Resistance Education (DARE) officers analyzed their prevention curriculum and highlighted those areas where the character concepts occur. Later in the year, a group of teachers developed activities for specific grade levels to teach the concepts as a part of the regular lesson. This will be an ongoing process to strengthen curriculum connections.

Preparing the Teachers

Recognizing that implementation strategies could only be effective if combined with a comprehensive staff development program, key instructional leaders identified and instituted a model of staff development. The members of the staff-development committee attended a trainers' workshop conducted by Dr. Philip Fitch Vincent, author of *Developing Character in Students* (1994). Dr. Vincent's Spokes of Character—rules and procedures, cooperative learning, teaching for thinking, reading for character and caring through service to others, are the basis of the model.

Staff-development workshops began in the spring of 1995. At this time, approximately 150 educators completed the ten-hour course. During that summer, Dr. Vincent conducted a four-hour workshop with the 72 principals, along with the same community members, curriculum supervisors, and school board members. Following this workshop, each building principal selected a person at the school to serve as the leader for character education. The lead contact persons attended a ten-hour training session. Some of the participants later taught the course for 450 educators who signed up the for the fall semester early-release staff development. Staff development is ongoing, either at the building level or as a part of the system-wide staff-development program.

 ## Mobilizing the Community

The task force established a public-awareness committee to coordinate community involvement through a community-wide campaign. The committee immediately coordinated a second summit to generate ideas. Approximately 350 people attended this summit and brainstormed activities at home, in the schools, in the religious community, in businesses and in the general community that promote the eight concepts. Once again, participants worked in small groups to come up with ideas and strategies.

The Public Awareness Committee compiled these ideas and produced a booklet for dissemination throughout the community. The committee appealed to the students to design a logo for the slogan "Celebrate Character in Cumberland County." The committee developed a campaign theme. It states:

Good Character

- Must start at home
- Must be taught
- Must be modeled
- Must be a united community effort
- Will lead to success!

The committee brainstormed other ideas and decided to have a mascot. After much thought and deliberation, the committee appealed to a panel of students to select an ambassador for character education. These students selected a bear because bears are appealing to young children and can represent either sex.

The committee planned a kick-off event to introduce the slogan, logo and mascot. Balloons, bands, cheerleaders and choral groups demonstrated ways to promote character to over 750 participants. Community leaders signed contracts to Celebrate Character in Cumberland County. Character Bear made its debut to the delight of the younger children. A "Concept of the Month" campaign was introduced to coordinate community involvement. The Cumberland County Medical Society Alliance and Sprint Carolina Telephone purchased and distributed books to third grade classrooms and the public library branches that addressed character development. Sprint Carolina Telephone company also provided funds for bumper stickers and pencils reflecting the character concepts.

Local ministers met to solicit the support of the church community. 75 religious leaders discussed ways they could promote the character concepts in their congregations. Some of the ministers dedicate a sermon each month to the designated concept for the month, children's church education programs emphasize the value of good character, and the ministers have funded a motivational speaker to hold assemblies at the eight high schools.

The public awareness committee also hosted a meeting of local radio program directors. Directors representing 13 stations attended. The directors discussed ideas they could use as a part of their broadcasts. As a result, the stations started airing public service announcements, featuring Character Bear at remote broadcasts and including information about the concept of the month in newsletters and children's publications.

The community actively supports the character education initiative. Bulletin boards, church marquees and businesses display the character concept of the month throughout the community. The Public Works Commission included an insert in its monthly billing that listed the concepts and ideas for parents. This was mailed to 77,000 homes. *The Fayetteville Observer-Times* publishes a quarterly insert called "Cumberland County Parent" that includes activities for children and adults to promote character. The Cape Fear Regional Theatre produced a show called the "Good Times Revue" based on the character education concepts. Students wrote essays, poems, short stories, and songs and they created dances and art to convey personal experiences. The theatre gave free performances for the schools and performed on the weekend for the public.

Spreading the Word

At the beginning of the 1995-96 school year, character education was a part of the superintendent's first systemwide goal: "Expand curriculum and character-growth opportunities to meet the needs of a diverse student population." The board of education included character development as a part of the required curriculum policy. The policy states that each student who graduates from Cumberland County Schools will learn to interact well and work cooperatively with others, and to demonstrate the ability to use the eight character concepts. All employees receive a monthly publication, and the message from the superintendent each month addresses the concept of the month. The lead contact persons at each school coordinate and report activities to the district coordinator. Assemblies, announcements, writing and reading assignments, incentives, newsletters and songs are some of the strategies used in the schools.

The definitions of the eight concepts were put into action statements and thus the code of character established. For example, the code for respect is "I will act with courtesy, tolerance and dignity." This code was published in a brochure, along with ideas for parents, and 75,000 copies were distributed to the schools so students could take them home, along with the existing code of conduct.

During the national Character Counts! Week in October, the schools and community hold special events. The Cumberland County Board of Commissioners, Fayetteville City Council and Cumberland County Board of Education all sign official proclamations recognizing the event. Letters to the newspaper editor and newspaper advertisements announce the observance of the week.

Cumberland County has been called upon to offer technical assistance to other school systems across the state. Presentations at professional organizations have established the program as a model.

Evaluating the Results

Determining the effectiveness of the character education initiative is a true challenge. Evaluation of character education programs attempts to prove that someone does the right thing when no one is looking! This is nearly impossible to assess. However, there are certain benchmarks that can be used to determine the impact of the program.

At this time, an evaluation plan is being designed. Statistics, such as the number of discipline referrals, short and long-term suspensions, attendance rates, and dropout rates, will be compared with the initial year of implementation. This analysis should give some indication of success.

Surveys will also be used to determine understanding of the concepts at the elementary level, and changes in behavior and perceptions at the middle and high school level. Parents and community leaders will be surveyed to determine the extent of public awareness and involvement. In the future, other approaches such as pre- and post-test measures will be designed for implementation.

 ## Maintaining the Momentum

Another challenge facing Cumberland County currently is to be able to sustain the energy and enthusiasm that has been generated in the past year. New ideas will continue to be explored. Lesson plans and activities to support the curriculum will be developed. Individual schools will determine ways to improve the school climate. The concept of the month campaign will continue. It is hoped that the idea of systematically developing character will continue to grow and become stronger.

 ## Closing Comments

Any change takes time. Those who introduce changes with the goal of having a significant impact upon our society must be patient. We must have the personal fortitude to stick with those principles in which we believe. Dr. Kevin Ryan, Director of the Center for the Advancement of Ethics and Character at Boston University offers *Ten Commandments of Character Education* (1995) for educators:

1. Thou shalt be a good example.
2. Thou shalt not carry this burden alone.
3. Thou shalt use the curriculum.
4. Thou shalt pay special attention to the hidden curriculum.
5. Thou shalt not surprise parents.
6. Thou shalt stick to the basics.

7.   Thou shalt use moral language.
8.   Thou shalt not reduce character education just to words.
9.   Thou shalt reward good character.
10. Thou shalt have a mandate for character education.

The time to teach and model the fundamentals of good character is now. The person who can truly make a difference in creating a positive environment where strong character can grow is you. *Good luck!*

References

Burrett, Kenneth, and Timothy Rusnak. *Integrated Character Education.* Bloomington, IN: Phi Delta Kappa Education Foundation, 1993.

Ryan, Kevin. "The Ten Commandments of Character Education," *The School Administrator,* September, 1995.

Vincent, Philip Fitch. *Developing Character in Students.* Chapel Hill, NC: New View Publications, 1994.

5 GREENFIELD, MA

The Responsive Classroom Approach Recognizes the Social Curriculum as a Cornerstone in Character Education

Chip Wood

CHARACTER EDUCATION IS INEXTRICABLY BOUND to the character of education. The most promising practices in character education are, not surprisingly, found in those schools that understand this maxim. However, many schools have initiated character education programs without a hard look in the mirror.

The character of education in any school is threefold:

1. The character of the curriculum
2. The character of the school climate, of rules and discipline
3. The character of the adult community

The Responsive Classroom[tm] is one professional development approach by schools to incorporate and integrate social and academic excellence throughout the entire school day. The Responsive Classroom provides a clear structure for teachers and administrators to work on all three facets of their school's character.

The Responsive Classroom addresses *the character of the curriculum* by helping teachers develop a more constructivist approach to teaching, by broadening children's range of choice in both academic process and content. It addresses *the character of the school climate, of rules and discipline* by providing clear structures for teaching social skills, engaging in proactive discipline strategies and maintaining school-wide and parental expectations around discipline issues. It challenges *the character of the adult community* by working with teachers, administrators and other school personnel to make room for new avenues for mutual support and meaningful conversations in the busy school day.

Schools in a variety of locales, from inner-city Washington, D.C., and Baltimore, Maryland, to suburban Cincinnati, Ohio, and rural Vermont have found Responsive Classroom strategies helpful in building a climate characterized by efficiency and competency in classrooms and corridors, lunchrooms and teachers' rooms.

The Responsive Classroom was developed by public school teachers, who in 1981 founded the Northeast Foundation for Children (NEFC) in western Massachusetts to foster positive change in public school approaches to curriculum development and school climate. For the past 15 years NEFC has worked with public school teachers while also operating a K-8 laboratory school and publishing books and materials for teachers.

The Responsive Classroom is based on the belief that the social curriculum in schools is as important as the academic curriculum and that academic excellence cannot occur without a strong foundation of social skills. This philosophy is strengthened in practice by over two decades of actual classroom teaching experience in developmentally appropriate settings by the lead trainers for NEFC.

NEFC provides Responsive Classroom workshops, semester-long university courses and summer institutes that strengthen teachers' foundations in child-development theory, essential to good teaching. Key to good teaching is the concept that social skills should be practiced with children with the same deliberateness as spelling or the times tables are practiced. The specific social skills of *cooperation, assertion, responsibility, empathy* and *self-control,* as identified by Elliott and Gresham (1990) are taught as cornerstones to acceptable student behavior and academic achievement. Teachers learn how to teach students these skills through modeling and role-playing, teacher reinforcement, reminders and redirection. Ruth Charney's widely acclaimed book, *Teaching Children to Care: Management in The Responsive Classroom* (1992) serves as a core text.

The Responsive Classroom has six basic components that can be utilized in the classroom at any grade level in elementary school:

1. **Classroom Organization** that provides for active interest areas for students, space for student-created displays of work and an appropriate mix of wholeclass, group and individual instruction.
2. **A Morning Meeting** format that provides children the daily opportunity to practice greetings, conversation, sharing and problem solving.
3. **Rules and Logical Consequences** that are generated, modeled and role-played with the children and that become the corner-stone of classroom life.
4. **Academic choice time** for all children each day that provides them with the necessity of taking control of their own learning in some meaningful way, both individually and cooperatively.
5. **Guided Discovery** of learning materials, areas of the room, curriculum content and ways of behaving that moves children through a deliberate and careful introduction to each new experience. There is no assumption that children already know how to do something before they begin.
6. **Assessment and Reporting to Parents** that is an evolving process of mutual communication and understanding.

The six components of The Responsive Classroom help teachers improve and strengthen their professional skills. Each component assists them in re-examining the work they do in the classroom from a critical vantage point. Teachers are asked to remember the enthusiasm with which they entered the teaching profession, filter it through their years of experience and then ask themselves the following questions in relationship to each component of The Responsive Classroom training they are receiving:

1. What is right for the children developmentally? That is, what tasks are age-appropriate for the children I am teaching from a physical, social, emotional and cognitive perspective?
2. How does each component foster the development of the key social skills of *cooperation, assertion, responsibility, empathy* and *self-control (CARES)?*
3. How am I using each component of Responsive Classroom to provide the critical balance in my classroom between teacher-directed learning and student-initiated learning, between whole group, small group and individual instruction, between an emphasis on products and process, and between competition and cooperation?

It is this third question that we hope alerts teachers to the potency and durability of The Responsive Classroom and its utility in their classrooms on a daily basis.

Research of Responsive Classroom initiatives (Elliott, 1995) supports the contention that the educational pendulum should not swing radically from one educational fad to another, but rather strike a critical balance of approaches. Achieving a balance is most apt to stabilize and improve classroom instruction and behavior, as well as strengthen achievement and character.

The Responsive Classroom, then, is not an add-on program or one more thing to be incorporated in an already frenetic school day. Rather it is a means for a teacher to focus on his/her professional growth and development and to internalize important conceptual understandings about teaching and learning. This allows for a more gradual change in the teacher's approaches to curriculum and students.

Each component of The Responsive Classroom provides teachers with the opportunity to address one or more of the characters of education each day in her classroom. For an example, let's look at what I called the first "character of education"—the character of the curriculum—in relationship to The Responsive Classroom component of "classroom organization." Through the lens of Responsive Classroom, the organization of classroom space, the schedule of daily activities and lessons, and the way transitions are accomplished all take on new meaning and importance.

Early primary teachers have long understood the need for well-organized learning centers in a classroom. Responsive Classroom training provides teachers with detailed structures for setting up such classrooms in ways that teach children how to manage both their learning and their behavior. Thus, the actual physical arrangement of the room becomes a management tool for both instruction and behavior.

Intermediate grade level teachers who are seeking to make their rooms and schedules more developmentally oriented are often confused about how to begin, because the only models available to them are at the primary level. When they see children in the early grades doing their work, they often cannot imagine how their students could function in such settings and how, as one teacher put it, "I'd keep them from playing all day."

The Responsive Classroom helps teachers at these levels understand the developmental needs of eight- through twelve-year-olds with special understanding for these children's growing ability to handle individual and group responsibility (Wood, 1994). Children in these older grades do not need learning centers to focus their studies or behavior, but they do need carefully organized and functioning supply areas that will help them nego-tiate working space in the room. They desperately need the responsibility for caring for paper, scissors, markers, microscopes and each other.

The second "character of education"—the character of the school climate, of rules and discipline—is at the core of The Responsive Class-room. Through the component of "rules and consequences," teachers are taught to re-focus their classroom discipline procedures away from pun-ishment and toward student ownership of realistic, real-life consequences for misbehavior. This change in approach is carefully taught in such a way as to help teachers spend time in their classrooms teaching discipline both proactively and reactively. Therefore, a good deal of classroom time is spent setting goals with students, establishing classroom rules and proce-dures together, and proactively teaching, through role playing and practice, how the rules are done, not just what they are.

Teachers employ logical consequences that require students to take a break from and eventually fix the situation they have created, or sometimes lose a classroom privilege for a period of time. The emphasis, once more, is on creating in the classroom a balance—that critical balance—between the external control of the teacher and the developing internal control of the student. Without the ability to practice this control in elementary school there is little chance that children moving into puberty and the struggles of adolescence will make good choices in their teenage years.

We have been asked to explore Responsive Classroom strategies with a number of middle schools. It is readily apparent that this need for a balance between external authority and the ability of students to practice self-control and responsibility in a school setting by being given some of that control is at the heart of character education for these grades especially. We have a long way to go to create structures that support this effort.

The third character of education—the character of the adult commu-nity—is, in our experience, the most challenging of the three characters to address. We are still learning how the implementation of The Responsive Classroom activates this third character issue in schools. Our work with thousands of teachers and hundreds of administrators in the last decade has brought us to the point where we recognize this issue is probably the crux of the matter. As in most professions, we in education have been focused largely on a "client-centered" approach. In school climate and discipline, therefore, we have found ways to look at and improve the ways students treat each other, and even the ways teachers interact with their students. We have created peer-mediation programs, character education programs, DARE programs and CARE programs.

We have done all this without really looking closely in the mirror. What is it like in the teacher's room? What kind of conversations occur there? How much pressure is there on one grade level of teachers to have their children "ready" for the next level of teachers? How often are teachers given time to plan together, to visit each other's classrooms as peer coaches? Where are the telephones for teachers located, if they exist at all? What is the physical space of teachers' rooms and planning spaces like? What does it say about the adult community? What happens after school? What are faculty meetings like? Who runs them and how do adults in the community resolve problems together? In other words, what is the climate of the adult community?

The teacher who can come to work tomorrow with the same enthusiasm she began her teaching profession with brings with her the character that provides the model for the students around her each day. In one school utilizing Responsive Classroom, faculty meetings are now held in a circle and mirror the Responsive Classroom component of "morning meeting," with teachers and administrators formally greeting each other, sharing news of their classrooms, engaging in affirmations and fun activities. In another, the principal and teachers entered a women's softball team in the summer recreation league and found they played together the way they wanted to teach together. In a third, substitute teachers are provided for teachers who want to participate in "Teacher Sharing Day" where teachers visit each other's classrooms to observe lessons or join in co-teaching a lesson, followed by time for discussing what they have experienced.

Developmental psychologists tell us that children need significance, belonging and fun to prosper emotionally and socially—to develop character. Adults, too, prosper in a workplace in which they feel safe, and important, and know they belong to a collective enterprise full of energy and support for the hard work they are doing. As we have come to realize more fully the importance of addressing this third character of education, we have refined The Responsive Classroom so it focuses more directly on developing the responsiveness of entire school communities.

In the last two years we have initiated The Responsive Leadership Forum, a collaboration of schools who are addressing all aspects of their community—from the playground to the lunch room, from the classroom to the teacher's room, from the hallways to the buses. These schools are providing training for their administrators, as well as their teachers, for their paraprofessionals and parents, as well as their children. These schools are finding ways to apply the African proverb to the living reality:

"It takes a whole school community to educate a school." Education must be social as well as academic, and it must teach us all to care.

About the Author

Robert (Chip) Wood, M.S.W., is a former elementary school teacher and principal. He is co-founder of Northeast Foundation for Children and Greenfield Center School, Greenfield, MA.

References

Charney, Ruth. *Teaching Children to Care, Management in The Responsive Classroom.* Greenfield, MA: Northeast Foundation for Children, 1992.

Elliott, Stephen N. *Caring to Learn, A Report on the Positive Impact of a Social Curriculum.* Greenfield, MA: Northeast Foundation for Children, 1993.

_____. *The Responsive Classroom Approach: Its Effectiveness and Acceptability.* District of Columbia Public Schools, 1995.

Gresham, Frank M. and Elliott, Stephen N. *Social Skills Rating System.* Circle Pines, MN: American Guidance, 1990.

Wood, Chip. *Yardsticks: Children in the Classroom, Ages 4-12.* Greenfield: MA: Northeast Foundation for Children, 1994.

6 ASHEVILLE, NC

Buncombe County Schools Nourish Promising Practices in Character Education which Foster Students' Achievements and Responsible Citizenship

Tom and Patsy Higdon

 It is a new year and Christmas break is over. As car riders approach the middle school for their first day back and as the first school bus arrives, students notice that the sign in front of the school has the new character trait highlighted—Character Trait of the Month— HONESTY. It is not long before they see and hear the first of the many times honesty and its meaning will be emphasized.

A large banner hangs in the lobby HONESTY—Being Truthful With Yourself and Others. The morning announcements include a reminder of what is meant by being truthful. The principal encourages everyone to refuse to lie, steal, cheat, deceive or take advantage of the trust of others. As the day begins in home rooms with Advisor/Advisee time, teachers introduce the new honor code that has been added to the school disciplinary plan. A lively discussion of how honor and honesty affect relationships and reputations is cut short by the first-period bell.

History

This is one example of many lessons on honesty seen in school classrooms in Buncombe County during the month of January as part of the Character Education Program begun in the fall of 1994. The Character Education Task Force was organized under the direction of the Assistant Superintendent for Instructional Services and the Health Education Coordinator of Buncombe County.

The task force was initially composed of teachers and administrators from elementary and middle schools in the six school districts along with central office representatives. It enthusiastically endorsed the need for schools to become active partners with families and their communities to develop good character in their youth. Additionally, the task force felt that an effective character education program would prepare students to become more responsible citizens and productive members of society, while helping make schools more civil, caring and academically sound.

After an examination of the available research and discussions with community leaders, the objectives of character education in Buncombe County Schools were established by the task force. The objectives were to enlist parents and other members of the community as full partners with Buncombe County Schools in the character-building effort; to provide instruction and guidance for Buncombe County school children on broadly supported traits of good character; and to develop an atmosphere in the schools which celebrates good character in all members of the community.

Parents and community members from each district were asked to join in the meetings of the task force in January, 1995. In this way the Character Education Task Force was able to obtain the grass-roots support necessary for successful implementation. A broad representation from the community included housewives, ministers, a public health worker, a consultant to the county commissioners, business leaders, industrial workers and a private industrial consultant.

The expanded task force identified character education needs and goals, selected the character traits it felt would be universally accepted in the community and planned methods for implementation. After this lengthy process throughout the 1994-95 school year, the foundation was laid which would ensure the support of a variety of constituencies for the program. The newspapers and public response have provided two such avenues of support.

The actual sequence of development used to expand the awareness of all the task force members was thorough. First, the participants of the task force were introduced to the history of character education. Then, exemplary programs and supporting research were reviewed, particularly the work of Thomas Lickona and Philip Vincent. Lickona's book, *Educating for Character (1991)* and Vincent's, *Developing Character in Students (1994)* were ordered for task force members to use as resource books. Dr. Vincent became a valuable consultant as well.

Next, tentative plans and goals for the Buncombe County program were developed, while teachers, administrators, students and parents identified a long list of possible character traits which could be included in the Buncombe County program. Eight character traits were finally selected to be emphasized in the K-8 schools. These were: respect, responsibility, honesty, courage, self-discipline, citizenship, caring and fairness.

After this, a report which contained the task force's recommendations was made to the superintendent and the Board of Education. The Board of Education expressed its strong support for the eight traits and for the plans that had been developed. In late summer of 1995, a teacher planning committee was organized which brainstormed possible implementation strategies for schools. The consensus in this thoroughly planned process was that character education should be integrated into the existing curriculum and not added on as an additional curriculum.

It was also agreed that faculties within each school should determine the most appropriate ways to incorporate the selected character traits in their schools. The vehicle for developing ownership of the character education program at the school level would be the School Improvement Team. This elected team of faculty, staff and parents, has been established in each school in North Carolina as a means for site-based management. These teams would be responsible for planning and assisting implementation at each school.

Implementation

Implementation of a character education program varied from school to school and from class to class, because plans were to be carried out within existing curriculum frameworks of each school. Following are anecdotal examples of how implementation might look in a middle or elementary school in the county.

The following journal entry is read by a third grader to the rest of the class:

> One day me and a few of my friends went to McDonald's to play on
> the playground. We started playing tag. Luckily I was not it. But
> then I saw a little boy about 2 or 3 years old and he was trying to
> get up to the tall place to get to the slide. So I decided to help him.
> I gave him a little nudge. I was careful not to hurt him. And just
> then the tagger came up and tagged me. But I didn't say anything.
> I just helped him go down the slide and then a good feeling was
> inside me that I had helped someone and I felt good about it.

The teacher notes that this student has obviously internalized the
character trait for December—Caring. She then uses the journal entry as
a prompt for further discussion on how caring looks and feels.

In January, middle school students progress through classes where
honesty is either the focus of the lesson or naturally integrated into the
regular academic lesson. One class has a community businessman discuss
the importance of working together in the world of work and being productive, honest, and responsible citizens.

The media center specialist has decided January would be the best
time to introduce plagiarism in his curriculum. The boys and girls begin
their P.E. lesson in basketball with an overview of what is considered
cheating or dishonest in this sport. A literature teacher is overheard
explaining that even fiction has an assumption of honesty and that there is
a difference between a lie and fiction.

A social studies teacher employs examples of propaganda used by
Hitler and Stalin to show the importance of honesty in government.
Additionally, the teacher accents that the citizens in a democracy have a
right to expect honesty in their elected officials. The day ends with the
last-period teacher handing out a card with honesty and its definition in
bold type. Homework instructions are given to keep the card on the refrig-
erator and to record incidents when the importance of honesty in family
life or peer relations are prevalent.

A similar scene at a nearby elementary school shows kindergartners
learning the letter H for Honesty and reading the story of "The Little Boy
Who Cried Wolf," then discussing why lying is wrong. A third grade class
reads a selection from the Junior Great Books series which will be used as
the basis for a seminar the next day. The story is "Ooka and the Honest
Thief," and the difference between borrowing and stealing is the main idea.

Many teachers may have decided to review the previous character
traits introduced throughout the county during September through
December before focusing on honesty. Bulletin boards are still seen

around the school that illustrate instances of responsibility, respect, citizenship, and caring. Thank-you notes are being read in several classes from senior citizen homes that were part of the classes' service projects on caring for the month of December.

One class is seen holding a meeting where students are in a circle, taking turns giving each other compliments for the times they have seen others show acts of kindness, respect or honesty. The faculty and staff even have a compliment board on which to pin a compliment card as recognition for someone who has been helpful or thoughtful. Again the character-trait-of-the-month card is given out at the end of the day. This way, parents will know what is being emphasized in order to teach and reinforce good character at home.

As seen from the examples of a possible day at an elementary or middle school, the core character traits chosen by the Character Education Task Force are being promoted and integrated into all aspects of school life and, we hope, at home as well. While a character trait may be emphasized each school month throughout the school system, all the traits are interwoven in expectations and actions throughout the school day in a comprehensive approach.

School Improvement Team chairpersons and principals received training to assist them in implementation at their school during the 1995-96 school year. The Character Education Task Force provided each School Improvement Team a resource packet with ample information to begin this process. The packet contained research articles, bibliographies of videos and books available in the county Media Center, along with task force recommendations. Character-trait cards were printed for Buncombe County students to take home each month. (One of the community task force members who owns his own printing business donated almost 50,000 character-trait cards and 3,000 brochures highlighting the character education program for use by students and parents in all K-8 schools.)

School Improvement Teams then made tentative plans for incorporating an emphasis on character education, which was written as an addendum to their School Improvement Plan. Each addendum included the school's present plan and plans for the future in five specific areas which had been outlined as the Spokes of Character (Vincent, 1994). The areas are: rules and procedures, cooperative learning, teaching for thinking, reading for character and service learning. Among the items listed in various schools' addenda were the following ideas.

Rules and Procedures

Developing and following good rules and procedures at school are essential steps in establishing a caring, learning environment in which students may develop the habits which lead to good character. Rules and procedures are implemented as teachers establish, post, and consistently enforce them. Establishing a homework policy or dress code are two such procedures. Students can help create class rules. Teachers can concretely model and teach specific rules, listing them positively and reinforcing them by acknowledging when students follow them. Schoolwide assembly and lunchroom-behavior guidelines use a universal symbol for silence. All expectations for rules and procedures are communicated to parents so they can help encourage students at home.

Cooperative Learning

Since learning to work and live cooperatively is critically important in life, students are expected to develop and improve their cooperative-learning skills. Through cooperative-learning experiences, students will develop caring attitudes and habits. Teaching cooperative-leaning skills and procedures requires an ongoing inservice to reach teachers who have not been trained. Heterogeneous and homogeneous groupings, followed by team-building activities, are used in different content areas. Pen pals with other schools, telecommunication projects, reading buddies, peer tutoring and classroom gardening are representative of experiences that promote co-operative learning. Extracurricular clubs and activities, such as Odyssey of the Mind teams or intramural sports, encourage working together.

Teaching for Thinking

Students must learn to think and reason as part of their school experiences. This skill is important not only in the academic world but also in the social demands of citizenship. Schools must work to ensure that students develop the thinking skills needed in this world by teaching study and higher-order thinking skills. The use of seminars, discussions, debates, analogies, science-process skills and open-ended questioning aid thinking and reasoning. It is important to treat all students as if they are gifted and to launch after-school projects such as Odyssey of the Mind, Chess Club, and Mathcounts as common components of school. Thinking skills are improved when students write, use story webbing and graphic organizers, and apply problem solving and research techniques in all content areas.

Reading for Character

Parents and educators have an obligation to provide literature for children which is uplifting and intellectually challenging. Quality literature and sound teaching strategies are used to reinforce and help students analyze the character traits which have been determined to be of value in the community. Strategies that encourage reading for character development include the use of Junior Great Books or books from Paideia reading lists for seminar instruction.

Teachers participate in adult seminars as well. Teacher and parent efforts are enhanced by having various people, including administrators and community members, read to students. Afterwards, the facilitators lead discussions with the students about their reactions to the positive character traits found in the literature. Journal writing after reading and discussion helps students express their own feelings about ethical and unethical situations in literature. Utilizing various types of literature, such as poetry and drama that emphasize good character, reading and discussing parables/fables and their morals, and discussing biographies of heroic characters of the past promote and enrich character education.

Service Learning

Buncombe County Schools is committed to having students engage in service opportunities within its schools and community because, in order to develop a caring attitude, one must reach out and touch other people. Projects such as across-grade-level buddy reading, peer tutoring or mediation, White Christmas, adopting a needy family, creating a clothes closet, or visiting senior citizens or the handicapped encourage students to reach out to others.

Service clubs like the Beta Club, a new-student welcoming committee, volunteer appreciation, or working for charity programs (like Jump Rope for Heart) also advocate caring. Celebrating Earth Day, recycling, endangered-animals protection projects, or school-beautification projects (like adopting an area of the school to keep clean) cultivate caring for our environment. Stressing random acts of kindness by recognizing or praising students when they help others may be one of the easiest and most productive techniques of service learning.

 ## Core Character Traits

While implementing strategies within the Spokes of Character, schools needed to know which character traits would be accepted by the community. The following traits were chosen and defined by Buncombe County's Character Education Task Force to be used and emphasized in the implementation process at each school. While each trait was designated a particular month for focus, they were all to be interwoven into the fabric of the school life and culture. The shorter statements were designed to be helpful for younger students and to be used on bulletin boards or banners. The elaborations were for designing the focus of lessons and for older middle school students.

SEPTEMBER

RESPONSIBILITY—Being accountable for one's actions. While we are accountable for our actions and decisions, we are also accountable for the results of those decisions and actions. Being dependable in carrying out obligations and duties.

OCTOBER

RESPECT—Showing consideration for self, others, property, the environment and the country. Understanding that all people have value as human beings. Our respect displays our belief in their importance and worth.

NOVEMBER

CITIZENSHIP—Showing respect, pride and allegiance for our country. Learning to function and participate in a democratic society. Making positive contributions to our school and community.

DECEMBER

CARING—Treating others with kindness and compassion. Acting out of concern and thoughtfulness for self, others and property. Being considerate, courteous, helpful and understanding of others. Treating others as you would like to be treated.

JANUARY

HONESTY—Being truthful with yourself and others. Refusing to lie, steal, cheat, deceive or take advantage of the trust of others.

FEBRUARY

COURAGE—The strength to practice positive character traits. The strength also to resist negative influences and remain steadfast in upholding ethical traits.

MARCH

FAIRNESS—Treating others in a consistent, impartial way (not playing favorites).

APRIL

SELF-DISCIPLINE—The ability to control oneself for the sake of improvement. Sticking to and following through on a commitment. Being in control of your words, actions, impulses and desires.

MAY

This month will be used by all schools to "celebrate" the successes of the school character education program, by reviewing each previous character trait and discussing the plans for the next school year.

 ## Evaluation

The following journal entry was read privately by the teacher of a third grader in Buncombe County. The class had been asked to write about any or all of the Three Rs they had been learning about as a part of their school's character education program.

The three R's respect, responsibility, and reasonable thinking they did affect me but not that much because this morning in the gym I shined the reflection of my watch in the teachers eyes and I wasn't very respectful and I haven't been very responsible because I haven't been keeping up with my homework.

This student had been asked to do a self-evaluation of her own character. Had she been using the Three Rs, which the whole school had been emphasizing during the beginning months of school? She decided she had not. Yet the teacher, in evaluating the effectiveness of the program, was very happy to see that even though the journal entry revealed its writer was not always acting upon what she had learned, at least she was very aware of what was expected of her. Upon further conferences with her, the teacher found that the student really did want to make better choices about her behavior.

Character education is an ongoing process for helping youth develop good character. Teachers have found character development difficult to evaluate within the relatively short time they teach their students, because the process is continuous, possibly even lifelong. While there are ways to evaluate character growth quantitatively over time, such as counting discipline referrals or the times students are caught being good, most evaluation so far has been subjective.

Probably the most common evaluation technique has been monitoring student behavior and noting if there has been overall improvement. Many teachers, when asked if they see improvements, make statements such as, "It's hard to tell because this is such a long-term process." Most have the attitude that anything we do "couldn't hurt!" Dr. Philip Vincent, the county's character education consultant throughout the planning stages, forewarned the task force that it could take at least three years before large results could be seen.

Parents can also be a source of information about the effectiveness of the program. In a parent survey at one school, 300 families responded. Only twenty of these did not know about the character education program of the school. Only three out of 300 believed that character education should not be taught at school and most expressed gratitude to the school for formally initiating such a program.

Comments were written such as, "It's a good program. It's about time schools went back to this type of thinking." Another said, "We are glad it is emphasized so that what we are trying to teach at home is reinforced at school." One parent got to the heart of why we must continue with this program by saying, "Particularly in light of the current 'normal' American household, I have nothing but praise and admiration for you for tackling this very important learning experience through school!" Buncombe County administrators intend to continue tackling character education to help guarantee the future successes of its students.

Systemwide evaluation plans include reviewing the number of tardies and absences. Also, surveys used by other systems will be examined to design a survey form for Buncombe County Schools. One prototype developed by the St. Louis School System asks questions regarding students' perceptions about the caring of teachers. Teachers' perceptions about the benefits of the program will also be assessed.

 ## Future Plans

Plans for the future of Buncombe County's Character Education Program are focused around refinement and involvement. Local schools will continue to find ways to fine-tune their programs as they implement their School Improvement Plan Addendum strategies. Resource and reference materials will be housed in classrooms, school media centers and the county media center. Several schools have plans to seek funding from grants to purchase more resources.

Each individual school was asked to submit a character education implementation plan to the Assistant Superintendent for Instruction. Those plans will be shared with all K-8 schools via an overview document so that schools might learn from each other. This will be an excellent method of expanding resources to all schools.

As this program progressed during this past school year, the task force co-chairs took pocket cameras into schools to photograph character education bulletin boards, along with student and staff activities which related to the implementation of the program. This pictorial "history" will be available for all schools to review as another method of educating, explaining and celebrating the first year's successes.

Plans are under way for getting more community input and involvement, as well as for moving the program into the six county high schools. The Buncombe County Commissioners appointed a Community Common Values Task Force, which has been seeking information from all sectors of the communities in the six school districts. Like the school system, this county task force has followed a plan which surveys the needs of the community and allows for meetings with various constituencies to find consensus on a set of values for the county.

The chairman of the Community Task Force met with the School System Task Force in the fall of 1995 in order to establish a framework in which the two groups could work together. One such joint effort was recently reflected at a district fire department, when the school system's monthly character trait appeared on a sign in front of the fire station.

Buncombe County's Character Education Program has grown from the vision seen at the first task force meeting into a countywide community effort. Its primary focus is to help young people understand, care about and act upon the core ethical traits valued by their community.

While the task force has always recognized that the initial responsibility for developing good character in a child belongs to the parents, its members acknowledge the significance of community members and school personnel supporting the parents' efforts to model and teach good character traits. The final results of this community effort aren't completely defined. However, everyone connected with the program has affirmed its role in making a more civil and caring community in which students not only achieve academically, but are becoming responsible and productive citizens. This result alone qualifies the character education effort to claim success.

ALBUQUERQUE, NM

Character Counts
at Bel-Air Elementary
in Albuquerque, New Mexico

Robin Saget

BEL-AIR ELEMENTARY SCHOOL, in Albuquerque, New Mexico, has created quite a stir in its innovative Character Counts program. Its involvement in this worthy endeavor led Albuquerque to establish itself as a "Character Counts" city and New Mexico a "Character Counts" state.

This public school, with a diverse student population, has 56 percent of its students participating in the free-lunch program. As a result, Bel-Air is a Title I school, receiving additional funding for remedial reading programs. The diverse population presented challenging student behavioral problems as well, steering the Bel-Air Elementary School's Restructuring Council to review the morale of its students and staff in September, 1991.

It was concluded that the staff and students felt unsafe in the school environment. The issue resurfaced in February, 1992, and by March, student behavior had plummeted even further. Positive interventions by teachers and parents proved non-effective. This safety issue was discussed at staff and grade level meetings, and parental involvement was sought in order to unify supportive forces and combat the decline in student and staff morale.

A School Climate Task Force was established in March. A Climate Audit Questionnaire was administered to assess the amount of confidence and trust within the school environment among students, staff and parents based upon specific behaviors. Student behaviors were identified by the severity of discipline referrals, the frequency of the student's visits to the counselor and concerns brought to the SRC. Staff behaviors were predicated on classroom and work environment observations, self-evaluation reports, parent-stated concerns and student evaluations. Parent behaviors were determined by parent-teacher conferences, counselor contributions and administrative information.

An analysis of the School Climate Audit revealed that students felt unsafe in the school's environment. The staff was uneasy with the lack of discipline, and the parents were fearful for their children's safety.

After the School Climate Audit Questionnaire was studied, an Analysis of Effectiveness in Group Work was administered through the SRC by The Albuquerque Public School Department of Research, Development and Accountability (RDA). The issues of trust, mutual support, communication, conflict resolution, utilization of resources, control methods and the environment's organization were researched. Favorable results pointed to a high degree of trust and mutual support among members. Communication, conflict resolution and the utilization of resources needed support, while control methods and the organizational environment were favorable. These assessment results assisted the task force in developing a school-wide plan for the coming year.

At the first meeting of The School Restructuring Council (SRC) of the 1993-1994 school year, the following questions were asked: "What do we want our students to look like? How do we want our students to act?" Also viewed was the Parent Perspective (derived from The Josephson Institute of Ethics): "How would we be described? How would we like to be described?" The results of the needs assessment and safety issues were discussed. The SRC brainstormed 36 words, some of which were compassion, boundaries, communication, respect, participation, trust, honest, safety, cooperation, flexibility, responsibility, forgiveness, consideration, courage, and willingness to risk.

Mr. Don Whatley, president of the Albuquerque Federation of Teachers, attended the SRC meeting in August. He told the Council of his involvement with Michael Josephson, founder of The Josephson Institute of Ethics and the Character Counts Coalition and the composing of The Aspen Declaration from which the six pillars of character evolved. The Council thought the six pillars—respect, responsibility, trustworthiness, caring, fairness and citizenship—complemented their 36 words and would be easier to incorporate into a common, consistent language of the school.

The Bel-Air Character Counts Task Force comprised of teachers from each grade level, the principal, assistant principal and the counselor was established at the next meeting. The goal of this program was to develop a school where teachers and students could feel safe in their bodies (physically), hearts (emotionally) and minds (intellectually). They needed to feel their bodies were free from physical violence; their hearts were open in order for them to express their needs; and their minds were free to process without fear of judgment. The Character Counts program would eventually include community components as well.

The Character Counts program was presented to the faculty in August, 1993, by the task force. A unanimous decision was made by the faculty to accept Character Counts as the mechanism to address the safety issue within the environment.

The task force made presentations to the staff and students. "The Word of the Month" was developed so that common, consistent language would be used throughout the school. Schoolwide assemblies presented The Word of the Month, a common definition for each pillar was established, enabling kindergarten through fifth grade students to comprehend each Word of the Month and the entire staff taught, spoke and role-modeled the chosen Word of the Month. The staff members examined their own behavior, being careful to present themselves as positive role models in utilizing the pillar throughout the school day.

The Respect pillar was addressed at the October assembly, led by task force members dressed as the California Raisins. They performed the Aretha Franklin song "R-E-S-P-E-C-T," whereby each "raisin" housed a letter from the word Respect.

Each letter took on a definition:

R = regard for others
E = exceptional people
S = self-awareness
P = politeness
E = esteem
C = courtesy
T = team work

The Raisins taught the definition of each letter; the counselor taught the idea of developing a safe school and feeling safe in our hearts, minds, and bodies; and the assistant principal offered sample lesson plans to the staff. A guest speaker from The Anti-Graffiti Coalition of the City of Albuquerque spoke on the concept of administering Respect into our community.

Caring was the pillar for the months of November and December at the assembly presentations. Each teacher chose a Student of the Month from their classrooms. This child was chosen on positive merits he/she displayed during the previous month when the pillar was Respect. The students were honored by receiving certificates signed by the principal and assistant principal.

Lesson plans were available to teachers to assist them in the teaching of the Caring pillar. A spokesperson from a local homeless shelter was the guest speaker. The children had been informed that this speaker would be attending the assembly so they agreed to bring canned goods for the homeless to the assembly. After the speaker's presentation, the student body gave the speaker over 400 canned goods for the shelter. The Word of the Month really came to life. *The Giving Tree,* by Shel Silverstein, was read at the assembly. As a result, a "Giving Tree" was set up in the cafeteria and decorated with paper hands from the students, thanking each other for their caring and sharing throughout Thanksgiving.

Integrating these six pillars into common, consistent vocabulary throughout the school day allowed the children to use the words and their meanings. Students were incorporating the pillars and language in their homes and community also. The transformation was extremely effective and apparent, even enhancing the literacy program. Activities within the classrooms, such as the writing and reading processes, reinforced the six pillars. Students were asked what the pillars meant to them. A fourth grade student, wrote this about Trustworthiness:

Ode To Trust

Trust you will keep for life,
but lying can cut through friendship like a knife.
Trust is good unless a secret is spoken,
if that happens,
trust is broken.

If trust is kept
you keep a friend,
and if you do,
fun's around the bend.
If you lose trust,
I feel I may bust.

If you don't believe what
I say is true,
ask my friends
they trust me too.

Another fourth grade student wrote this poem about Fairness:

Life is not fair because people lie.
Life is not fair because people kill.
Life is not fair because there are riots.
Life is not fair because people can be prejudiced.

Life is good because people go to church.
Life is good because people meet people,
Life is good because people learn.
Life is, because we are here.

Other schoolwide activities were being formulated. The back wall of the playground was painted with six pillars words, replacing unsightly graffiti. Further celebration of the pillars was expressed in muslin banners, made by each grade level, being hung on the front gate. They were later moved to the cafeteria for permanent display. Pictures, posters and literature focusing on the six pillars of character were placed throughout the school's halls. Literature trade books were purchased and shared. The six pillars became the foundation for the Mediation Conflict Resolution Program. The school's discipline procedures and classroom rules were rewritten to address the six pillars.

Launched by a parade, the City of Albuquerque added Character Counts to its philosophy. This initiative was supported with city funding. All Albuquerque public school students attended the parade. The Bel-Air school body and staff wore T-shirts displaying the six pillars. Bel-Air Elementary was recognized as being the first school in New Mexico to be a Character Counts school. The school reported the progress of the

Character Education program to the parents and community in monthly newsletters.

In March, 1994, U.S. Senator Pete Domenici, representing New Mexico, attended the monthly Word of the Month assembly. He offered words of encouragement and recognition for the school program. In April, New Mexico Governor Bruce King entered Bel-Air's achievements into the Congressional Record in Washington, D.C. Hence, the local and national news media joined the Character Education movement to increase the public's awareness of the viability of such programs.

The community's participation affirmed the school-wide effort to make Character Count! City-wide school marquees proclaimed The Word of the Month. The Join-a-School partners pledged their commitment to Character Counts by participating and cooperating. The school started receiving telephone inquiries about the Word of the Month idea. The callers were concerned about teachers teaching ethics. Some comments were, "Who are you to teach my child ethics? Don't you know there is a separation of church and state? Why don't you stick to reading and writing?" The school's spokespersons informed the inquirers that the Bel-Air staff was not teaching religion or morals. Rather, the students were being taught to be respectful, responsible, trustworthy, fair and caring citizens. The community's citizens accepted the Character Counts concept totally after being asked "Which one of these pillars do you not want your child to possess?"

At the end of the 1993-94 school year, the Bel-Air students, staff and parents evaluated the Character Counts program. The responses were compiled by The Department of Albuquerque Public School Research, Development and Accountability (RDA).

On a 10-point scale, 10 equaling "I think it's great; let's expand it," the respondents averaged 9.5. Several evaluators assessed this project as "among the most important things we've done."

"Did the efforts affect student behavior in the classroom?" was also asked. If 10 equaled "the focus on student character development improved their behavior immensely," those filling out the survey rated the current effects at an average of 8.1. Some replies pointed out that extremely problematic students still misbehaved, but that many in the school were now better able to discuss behavior problems when they occurred.

A similar 10-point scale was used to measure student behavior outside the classrooms. The average rating was 8.2. Respondents indicated that children were more aware of what constituted irresponsibility and that, consequently, there were fewer discipline "slips" since the program was initiated. From August to October 1993, 47 discipline slips were issued to students for displaying disrespect for others and property. In December, this number was drastically reduced to twelve.

"Had relationships among staff members at Bel-Air changed at all?" was another question asked. With 5 equaling "about the same" and 10 equaling "much improved," staff responses indicated that there had been mostly positive changes, with the average rating being 8.1. Several commented that the faculty was "more trusting and caring," while very few described them "horrible like last year."

"Were more in-services needed to better implement this program?" was the final question. About two-thirds of the participants wanted to see either a few more hours devoted each month or additional staff and parents involved. Other suggestions included time for sharing ideas, dissemination of a bibliography for each pillar and parent-education classes.

In general, those returning the survey felt that "the response to this program was amazing" and urged "fostering its continuance." While the staff originally felt uneasy about the newness of the program, they gradually recognized its merits and could see the dramatic changes in the school.

The parents' and students' assessments of the *Character Counts* program at Bel-Air were equally as positive, with virtually everyone deeming the pilot project worthwhile. The only exception was eight percent of fourth and fifth graders, and two percent of parents who found the program "not important" or "not worth pursuing."

Even though some fourth and fifth graders had difficulty expressing what they knew, or declined to complete such forms, the remaining 70 percent clearly demonstrated their understanding of the character words. The survey gave students the opportunity to define four character traits which had been featured in the school's program. Interestingly enough, fourth graders seemed to be more adept at this task than fifth graders.

The survey made inquiry about any changes in students' behaviors, both individually and peer-related, as a result of the new Character Counts program. While 19 percent said they "didn't know," 87 percent of those who did have an opinion thought peer behaviors had changed. One fifth grader summed it up, "I think Character Counts is changing our school in good ways." Although a significant 45 percent responded that they "don't know" about their own behavior, 68 percent testified to changes in themselves they attributed to what they had learned through the program.

Reporting that their children had talked "some" or "a lot" about the program were 72 percent of the parents sampled. Similarly, 85 percent related that their children had mentioned "some" or "a lot" of at least one of the four pillars that had been introduced. While 91 percent noticed the "advertising" of the program on the marquee in front of the school, 76 percent had read about the program in the newspaper or the school news-letter. Parents who had heard their children mention the *Character Counts* certificates and awards program equalled 72 percent, with 57 percent re-vealing their children talked about what they had learned in school assem-blies and classrooms.

Perhaps the most encouraging statistic of all was that 21 percent of parents saw no change in their own children's behavior that might have been a result of the program, because these children already exhibited these traits before the program's inception. Another 57 percent saw "few" attributable changes and 21 percent saw "many"! A parent's comment spoke for several: "I'm glad that (child's name) is going to a school where there is serious effort to build a healthy environment."

After all the evaluations and assessments, the *Character Counts* program was firmly in place for the 1994-95 school year. The City of Albuquerque began to implement *Character Counts* into the community and businesses. Thirty-six community and business people, along with Albuquerque Public School employees, attended a three-day training led by Michael Josephson.

Yet, in spite of all the best efforts of school personnel and commu-nity participants, discipline began to regress at Bel-Air the second year of the *Character Counts* program. Problems that once had been a part of our school's environment began to resurface. The task force met with the SRC and reviewed the situation. Staff changes were a factor; the school's assis-tant principal and counselor were now half-time. The newness of the program had worn off. The staff was not as energetic about the program, because the attention was now being focused on the school district and other schools' successes. Media attention had moved on. The language of the program was not being used, and the importance of oral reinforcement and praise was mostly forgotten. New students were attending Bel-Air with no prior background knowledge of the program. Also taken into account were the scarcity of visual aids, the lack of full-time discipline procedures and consistent consequences, as well as holding students accountable for their behavior choices. Discipline slips, which totaled six in August, had risen to 29 by October. Role-modeling had relaxed. Too few incentive pro-grams contributed to the backsliding in the Character Counts program.

It was the consensus of the task force that this program had to be handled with consistency and taking this program for granted was not an option. The continuation of this program was vital for staff and student safety. A staff meeting was called and these concerns were voiced. The staff and faculty were reminded of the commitment to the program and the need for consistent, positive role-modeling. Was the energy still present to continue with the program without the previous year's accolades and recognition? It was agreed that the necessity of this program was unquestionable. The positive outcome of the program was apparent. Support groups were formed and the school's discipline policy was rewritten to incorporate the six pillars.

Incentive began to flow back into Bel-Air. In December, the discipline slips numbered six. The school rules were reviewed daily in classrooms. Announcements included student and staff responsibilities for displaying character. Respect, responsibility, caring, fairness, trustworthiness and citizenship resurfaced at Bel-Air.

The 1995-96 school year is the third year for the Character Counts program at Bel-Air. There has been consistent reinforcement and explanation of the six pillars in assemblies, schoolwide language and classroom focus. New students and teachers are familiar with the program. In August, the discipline slips totaled 11; in January they numbered 12. At-risk students are being guided by mediators and teachers. The staff and student body are being responsible for educating the population. The Bel-Air Task Force is still in place. Each grade level has adopted a pillar and has accepted the responsibility of teaching The Word of the Month at assemblies. The task force is available to assist the grade level as needed. The program adopted for "safety" issues at Bel-Air Elementary School in Albuquerque, New Mexico, has now become a nationwide endeavor.

All Albuquerque Public Schools (APS) are now encouraged to implement Character Counts into their environment. Schools are being trained by the Michael Josephson trainers. An APS Task Force and trainers support group have been established. Future Josephson Institute trainings are being scheduled.

The Character Counts program works because of its simplicity. The common, consistent language is easily learned, spoken and role-modeled. The crisis that Bel-Air encountered is being addressed by returning to the basics of individual and community character development. It is known that the common, consistent teaching, role-modeling and practice of the program are vital for its success. "Walking the Talk" is essential for the ongoing success of the program.

Helen Keller once spoke these words of inspiration: "I am only one, but I still am one. I cannot do everything, but still I can do something; and because I cannot do everything, I will not refuse to do the something that I can do. I wondered why somebody didn't do something, then I realized that I was somebody." CHARACTER DOES COUNT!

8 INDIANAPOLIS, IN

School Improvement Planning Teams Initiate Character Education into the Curriculum in Metropolitan School District of Lawrence Township

Duane E. Hodgin, Ph.D.
Lauretta Holloway
Linda Knoderer
Gordon Mendenhall, Ph.D

 ## History

The Metropolitan School District of Lawrence Township in Indianapolis, Indiana, is located in a residential suburb of nearly 100,000 people. The school district's enrollment is over 14,000 students and is one of only twelve growing school districts in Indiana. The district is growing at a rate of 300-400 students annually. Students represent racially and economically diverse backgrounds Approximately 24 percent of the students are African-American, 1 percent are Asian and Hispanic, with the remaining percentage being Caucasian.

The Lawrence Township School District is recognized as a "lighthouse school district" throughout Indiana and the Midwest because of its innovative and cutting-edge programs. Lawrence Township has two high schools, three middle schools, nine elementary schools (three of which are choice magnet schools), a centralized kindergarten with 870 students and a vocational career center. Seven of the schools, including both high schools and a middle school, have been recognized as "Blue Ribbon Schools of Excellence" by the United States Department of Education.

The character education initiative in the Lawrence Township schools has gradually evolved since 1983, with the focus on developing qualities of respect, responsibility and self-discipline in the students. All schools established School Improvement Planning Teams which were initially funded by a grant from the Indiana Department of Education.

School Improvement Planning Team workshops were conducted by the Lawrence Central High School and Lawrence North High School faculties and administrative staff in 1985. The issue discussed was "What can be done to address the decline in respect and courtesy and manners demonstrated by many students?" From this meeting and a series of faculty-led in-service programs, the idea of the "Focus of the Week" was originated, which is a character message that is presented over the PA system to the entire student body. Vic Bardonner, a Home School Advisor at the time, was instrumental in developing the Focus of the Week concept. The Focus was a short phrase emphasizing consideration, courtesy, respect for self and others and rights and responsibilities. It was also posted in each classroom, and teachers agreed to provide follow-up on the focus through-out the week. The follow-up took on many creative forms such as "bonus questions" on quizzes and tests, class discussions and writing assignments.

Since 1985, Lawrence Central's Focus of the Week has remained effective. New video technology and television monitors in each class-room allow the presentation to be viewed on television. A planning team of staff, administrators and students has replaced the original individual teacher as the creator of the weekly focus. The student members play a key role in developing and producing each Monday's focus.

Focus topics encourage students to think about a message or issue, usually centered around the character traits that were identified earlier. Some focus topics deal with timely social issues such as violence, gangs, sexual harassment, drugs, and drinking and driving.

Each year a schoolwide theme is developed and a large banner with the theme is displayed in the student commons and is reinforced in the class-rooms. The core tenets of each year's theme concentrate on integrity, respect for self and others, honesty, trust, decision-making and responsibility.

Lawrence Central High School's theme and banner for the 1995-96 school year is "Unity in Our School Community." The Student Congress, a representative group of the student body, meets regularly and serves as a sounding board and conduit to discuss issues about student and staff honesty, respect, courtesy, integrity, honoring differences and cooperation. Beginning in the 1995-96 school year, Student Forums—Things That Matter were scheduled four times. The Student Congress helped to determine the topics for discussion.

Many of the schools have also adopted themes with character-related components. Numerous speakers, in-services and workshops have involved teachers, administrators, students and parents in various kinds of awareness and training opportunities. These activities have focused on dignity, respect for differences, caring, responsible decision-making, critical-thinking skills, cooperative learning and problem-solving, as well as a host of other topics and issues that are a part of character education and development.

It is also noteworthy that the school district's Strategic Plan has adopted as one of its basic beliefs, "Schools will reflect community needs and aspirations and will nurture in students a sense of responsibility to the school and community." In the subsequent years, all 15 schools in our district have included character education as an integrated component of the curriculum and daily school activities. This is reflected in our district and school mission statements and in our Board-adopted Human Dignity Policy.

 ## What We Are Presently Doing

For well over a decade, our school district has been involved in some component of character education and development even though it might not have been categorized as such. Identifying the need for character education in such an informal manner 13 years ago became the focal turning point at both of our high schools. Character education has continued to evolve in such a way that all of our schools infuse it into the curriculum through a variety of ways.

Our students are introduced to character education beginning at the kindergarten level. The Centralized Kindergarten, consisting of 870 students, is a specially designed school that is developmentally appropriate for the 5- to 7-year-old child. All teachers are trained in early childhood education and are knowledgeable of early childhood research. This unique school is one of only a few district-wide self-contained kindergarten programs in the state. It is also the only kindergarten in Indiana that is certified by the National Association of Education for Young Children (NAEYC).

Principal Barbara Stryker and the Centralized Kindergarten staff members have worked for more than ten years in developing and refining school procedures and disciplinary processes, student behavior expectations, and school routines and traditions. The theme for the Centralized Kindergarten, "We Believe in Children," is proudly displayed on a beautiful banner to greet students and parents as they enter the school. Within the last three years, the staff has incorporated the MegaSkills and Lifelong Guidelines and has developed the "I Care rules." (Hands are for helping, not for hurting; Use quiet voices; Use I Care talk; Use walking feet.) All of these are visible in classrooms in a variety of creative ways.

The I Care rules, which are tied to character traits, are used in the classrooms, in the halls, on the bus, on field trips or at special activities, and the Student Support Specialist uses the I Care rules when working with children in student groups and in disciplinary situations. The teachers and instructional assistants reinforce behavior that is consistent with the MegaSkills, Lifelong Guidelines, and I Care rules' character traits. Teachers and the Student Support Specialist also use books and stories to promote character education and development (e.g., The Brute Family, Sofia and the Heartmender, Responsibility, Skillstreaming, etc.)

The Centralized Kindergarten is a place where all children are exposed to character education in a developmentally appropriate manner throughout a variety of procedures, activities, rules, traditions and rituals. The climate is vibrant, exciting, nurturing and rewarding.

Susan Brash is a 1995 National Distinguished Principal at our Amy Beverland Elementary School, which is one of our U. S. Department of Education's National Blue Ribbon Schools of Excellence. Under Ms. Brash's leadership, the entire staff has been trained in Dorothy Rich's MegaSkills and Susan Kovalik's Integrated Thematic Instructional (ITI) Model. Teachers use thematic instruction throughout all grade levels as well as the Cooperative Learning Model of Johnson and Johnson. The school now serves as a local, state and national training site for "How to Create a Brain Compatible Classroom and School." Many of our teachers at the elementary, middle and high school level have been trained by the Amy Beverland principal and teachers.

The community developed a mission statement which became the constitution for the Amy Beverland School family: "The Amy Beverland family is committed to academic excellence and the cultivation of individual potential through a cooperative, enriched environment where each person feels equally significant and appreciated." To formalize this mission, the following beliefs were developed and are practiced by the entire school family:

- The five Lifelong Guidelines of Truth, Trust, Active Listening, No Put Downs, and Personal Best.
- The ten MegaSkills of Confidence, Motivation, Effort, Responsibility, Initiative, Perseverance, Caring, Teamwork, Common Sense and Problem-solving.
- A Brain Compatible School evidenced by Trust and an Enriched Environment, Meaningful Content, Adequate Time and Choice.
- Joy is shared and grief is divided.
- Educating everyone takes everyone.
- As good as we are, we can get better.

These six beliefs, along with the mission statement, form the basis of the school's character education program. The ten MegaSkills and the Lifelong Guidelines are taught and reinforced during the year by each teacher and other school staff members.

Character education at Amy Beverland, as in our other schools, is incorporated into the total curriculum as a means to academic excellence for everyone. This systems approach to learning at Amy Beverland is where every stakeholder has a part in ensuring that the climate, culture and curriculum work in tandem to achieve the mission for everyone. The mission statement, the MegaSkills and the Lifelong Guidelines are posted in every classroom, the cafeteria, on the school buses and are even sent home to parents, asking them to post them on their refrigerators.

Teachers integrate the Lifelong Guidelines through Target Talk (labeling behavior), literature, cooperative-learning activities, community circles, school rules and discipline procedures, class meetings and, most important, through staff modeling. Student Support Specialists at every elementary school organize student support groups which practice making decisions and responsible choices, problem-solving, conflict resolution, anger management, and getting along with others. Additional groups are facilitated depending upon the need.

Staff at Amy Beverland also develop an annual theme, but the message is consistently attuned to the specialness of "all school family members." Examples of these family themes are "Celebrating a Family of Believers," "Celebrating Diversity in Our Family," and "Celebrating Our Tapestry of Talents." A few years ago, we used a district-wide theme and even had T-shirts made that promoted the message of character education. The theme was $E=MC^2$ (Everyone Must Care, Too).

Another schoolwide program, called "Respect and Responsibility,"
(R & R) was implemented by Lauretta Holloway at Indiana Creek
Elementary, one of our magnet schools. The R & R program is a wholistic
and systematic approach to character education and development which
was encouraged and supported by former principal Dr. Karen Gould, and
present principal Rebecca Shermis. Teachers met at the beginning of the
1994-95 school year to agree upon six important life skills that would
benefit all children. All staff members received in-service training on the
program components in the spring of 1995 and agreed to use the R & R
program in their classrooms.

As part of the R & R program, the principal talks to all students via
the intercom twice a week at the beginning of the day. The message
addresses respect and responsibility issues which include a variety of character education components. Teachers followup with specific mini-lessons
and teachable moments to reinforce the six "Life Skills" which are:

- We respect others.
- We respect property.
- We are responsible for our actions.
- We are truthful.
- We show our personal best.
- We are active listeners.

Each week parents receive suggested activities that support the
principal's message and the teachers' mini-lessons.

The Life Skills and the "Five Basic Principles of Respect and
Responsibility" (listed below) are posted in classrooms and on all Indian
Creek School buses.

- I am responsible for everything I do.
- I am responsible for getting my own education.
- I am responsible for treating all persons, my family members
  and others everywhere with respect and consideration.
- I am responsible for supporting my community/nation/world.
- I am responsible to the earth, that I treat it with loving care, pre-
  serving it for all time.

The Student Support Specialist teaches life skill lessons in all classrooms throughout the year. High school peer facilitators work with
selected students once a week.

At another elementary school, Skiles Test Elementary principal
Judie King and her staff use the acronym PRIDE (Preparing Responsible

Individuals in a Diverse Environment) as their theme and focus. Each school day begins with individual students leading their peers in the "PRIDE Pledge." (Put-downs are prohibited; Respect and trust toward one another; Insist upon your personal best; Discuss and listen actively; Expect and give truth and honesty.)

Principal Cathy Dyer and staff members of Mary Castle Elementary School were one of our first schools to embrace the DARE program (Drug Awareness Resistance Education). This program, taught by local police officers to all fifth grade students, focuses on problem-solving and responsible decision-making skills.

At the middle school level, all three middle schools use the MegaSkills and Lifelong Guidelines as part of their character education focus. Each middle school has a theme. For example, at Craig Middle School, the staff and Principal Bill Gavaghan, adopted the theme and acronym CARE (Communicating, Accepting, Respecting, and Encouraging). A large CARE banner greets students, staff and visitors at each of the schools' two main entrances.

The emphasis on character education at our two high schools is reflected by teaching strategies that include cooperative learning, critical thinking and an analysis of character issues in literature and social studies. Each high school is also active in community/service learning projects that involve classrooms and clubs. These service activities include: peer tutoring programs, recycling and ecology programs, peer-conflict management, National Honor Society service requirements for membership and peer facilitators, food and clothing drives, as well as others.

During the Rodney King trial a few years ago, two all-school forums were held to discuss issues and concerns. The forums were led by students and specific ground rules were established for the dialogue. The ground rules focused on respect for others' opinions, showing respect to other speakers, open-mindedness, taking turns and not personalizing differences of opinion.

School administrators periodically make video recordings throughout the school year to address issues regarding student behavior and expectations. These videos reinforce the positive things students do, as well as talk about concerns involving student behavior. Two videos made during the first part of the 1995-96 school year included showing respect for the flag and inappropriate student language in halls. Other video presentations have included sportsmanship at athletic events, proper etiquette at assemblies and performing arts events, respect toward others demonstrated by actions and appropriate dress, as well as a video explaining the significance of Veterans' Day. After each video showing, teachers follow-up with a class discussion.

Individual teachers throughout the township have promoted the development of good character in their students in a multitude of ways. One such teacher, Dr. Gordon Mendenhall, a biology and genetics teacher at Lawrence North High School, has been particularly active in developing and implementing classroom strategies, conducting in-service presentations, and working with school-improvement committees to implement programs that support character development. Dr. Mendenhall's academic strengths are in human genetics and bioethics, and he has attempted to forge this academic content with character development and decision-making skills.

Since the early 1980s, he has used his in-service academic training in human genetics and bioethics, provided by the National Science Foundation, to incorporate ethical decision-making into a human genetics course taught first at both Lawrence Central and Lawrence North High Schools and presently at Lawrence North High School. In 1988, he conducted in-service presentations at Lawrence Central to help facilitate the use of discussions about character development and ethical decision-making as an educational strategy. This in-service instruction supported the Focus of the Week program and raised awareness of character issues among the faculty members. The human genetics course was recognized by the National Association of Biology Teachers (NABT) as one of 20 exemplary programs that successfully explore the interface of science, technology and societal issues.

More recently, Dr. Mendenhall has implemented teaching activities designed to create an ethical classroom—a classroom where students explore the decision-making process and in doing so become more reflective and critical thinkers. One of his students, Alicia Schultz, stated, "The Decision-Making Model we learn in Dr. Mendenhall's genetics class is a tool that teaches and encourages students to devise a model that identifies the fundamental criteria for making a good decision. The process can be used throughout life as difficult decisions arise. Students are more likely to make better choices as a result of the model we learn."

Dr. Duane Hodgin, Assistant Superintendent for Educational Support Services initiated a special character education/awareness activity during the second semester of the 1995-96 school year. He and Linda Knoderer, Administrative Assistant for Educational Support Services, visited three elementary schools, two middle schools and both high schools within the school district. The character education/awareness presentation was done in 21 classrooms, grades 4-12, involving over 500 students.

The purpose of the presentation was to assess how students perceive what character means to them, what they define as character, how they feel that character is modeled in their school, who they view as positive character models and what they think should be done to increase character education in their schools.

The information shared by the students was analyzed by our Character Education Planning Team. The team consists of Dr. Hodgin, Lauretta Holloway, Linda Knoderer and Dr. Mendenhall, all of whom who attended the Character Education Training In-service conducted by Dr. Philip Vincent.

After analyzing the results, the team used the information to help plan for the in-service to be conducted in the fall of 1996. A summary of the results will be shared with the principals, superintendent, and the Board of Education. Beginning in September, 1996, a districtwide Character Education Planning Team will be convened to further explore how teachers and administrators can enhance character education activities within their schools and classrooms. Representatives of the committee will include teachers appointed by the Lawrence Education Association, administrators, parents and community members.

How We Are Evaluating the Effectiveness of our Character education Efforts

Evaluating the effectiveness of our character education initiatives has been done in a variety of ways. These include informal personal feedback from staff, students and parents, as well as more formal written surveys. At Lawrence Central High School, the School Improvement Planning Team and the North Central Accreditation Steering Committee have chosen character goals as a school priority for more than eight years.

All of our schools perform periodic school climate audits (written and verbal responses) which help to assess student, staff and parental attitudes and responses to many school related issues, including character education. The North Central Association and our state Performance Based Accreditation self-studies also examine the attitudes and behaviors of the students, staff, administration, parents and the community. Staff members and administrators consistently communicate with each other regarding the working relationship with students, staff members and parents.

Our character education efforts and initiatives are addressed and reviewed every year by each school's School Improvement Planning Team. As is true of all evaluation, it must be an ongoing process that involves both formative and summative procedures. Empirical data regarding character education's effectiveness is difficult to collect; our school district is seeking ways to do a better job in this area. There are good instruments available which we hope to adopt and use in the future. Perhaps the overall best indication of character education's effectiveness is how students and staff, on a daily basis, relate to and respond to one another.

Examples include a teacher who commented, "Many students are struggling with their 'character' at this age. Dr. Hodgin's presentation to the class helped the students to define and better understand what 'good character' is. The students were able to identify descriptive words and phrases that relate to a person's character." A parent commented, "I strongly support this character education effort, as I feel that many of our students are not receiving this training at home. I think the schools should be spending more time and effort on character development. If you are seeking additional input or volunteers, I would be interested."

 ## What Are Our Future Plans?

Future plans, beginning with the 1996-97 school year include the following considerations:

- Develop a districtwide committee to further assess the present programs and generate new practices and activities that we could be doing in all of our schools to more effectively infuse character education into the curriculum and activities.
- Develop a districtwide character theme and banner to hang in our central office, include on our school letterhead and in each school (e.g.,"Intelligence plus character—that is the goal of true education."—Dr. Martin Luther King)
- Have all schools, through their School Improvement Planning Teams, consider schoolwide themes and banners that bring focus to the school's character education efforts.
- Institute a character-assessment instrument that will measure the impact of our programs.

- Have each school review its mission statement to see if it reflects the moral/character development of students.
- Develop an in-service program on "Character Education: What It Is Not, What It Is and What It Can Be." The audience would be the entire administrative team—all counselors and Student Support Specialists, department chairpersons, middle school team leaders, selected teachers from each school and student, parent and community representatives. This is planned for fall of 1996. It will also be videotaped for use at faculty meetings.
- Develop a Character Education Policy similar to the Human Dignity Policy.
- Encourage the infusion of character traits/components into instructional practice on a districtwide basis.

"Character is revealed by what one thinks about and how one feels and behaves toward others. It is an inside-out expression of who we are and what we and what others believe ourselves to be."
—Dr. Duane Hodgin

Authors

Duane E. Hodgin, Ph.D.
Asst. Superintendent for Educational Support Services
Lauretta Holloway
Student Support Specialist, Indian Creek Elementary
Linda Knoderer
Administrative Assistant for Educational Support Services
Gordon Mendenhall, Ph.D.
Genetics/Biology Teacher, Lawrence North High School

9 DAYTON, OH

The Allen School Experience: A Story of Transformation

Rodolpho S. Bernardo
Principal

Background

The Allen School Experience is a story of transformation. In a period of three years, the staff at Allen witnessed improvement in students' test scores by 49 percent, reduced suspensions by 93 percent, increased parent involvement in PTA by thirty-fold, and bettered teacher attendance, which ranked among the highest in the district. The entire staff contributed to the creation of a learning organization at Allen. We examined our ways, made continual changes and learned from our experience in the process of transforming the school's learning environment.

Allen is an elementary school in northeast Dayton, Ohio, with 537 students in kindergarten through sixth grade. It has a staff of 28 certified teachers, eight paraprofessionals, and six special or part-time teachers. The school draws students from all of Dayton.

Appointed as the third principal in one year in January, 1989, I observed that the lack of order made it difficult to create a learning environment. The test scores (36.5 NCE on standardized California Achievement Tests) were near the bottom in the district (ranked 28 out of the 33 elementary schools) and significantly below the national norm.

In 1989, 78 percent of the students were receiving Aid for Dependent Children, and 59.5 percent came from single-parent homes. Sixty percent were African-Americans, 39.5 percent Euro-Americans, and .5 percent of other parentage. This same year marked a period of great transition for Allen, which was first reorganized from a K-2 neighborhood school to a K-6 classical/traditional magnet school. Then, Allen was selected to participate in a site-base management program.

 ## The Transformation

Many years of being a classroom teacher finally led me to the promotion of principalship at Allen School in 1989, which added another change to this transition period. My initial excitement as the new principal of Allen was quickly doused right from the first day. I experienced quite an awakening.

When those yellow buses arrived in the morning, bus drivers handed me several referral forms naming students who were fighting and causing problems on the bus. Students would come up to me saying, "He pushed me," or "She kicked me," or "Jaimie was cussing and threatening Cleo." So before the day began, students were lined up in the office to be disciplined. Then, after the school bell rang, more students were referred to the office from classrooms whose teachers could not handle them. Next, the phone rang with an angry parent yelling at me because their child was mistreated by another student and we hadn't done anything about it.

Ten students (on average) with undesirable behavior were referred to my office each day in 1989. Now, the teachers refer the best students to the principal's office to be recognized for their good performance.

Jack Mezirow, in his book *Transformative Dimensions of Adult Learning,* says:

> Perspective transformation involves a sequence of learning activities that begin with a disorienting dilemma and concludes with a changed self-concept that enables a reintegration in one's life context on the basis of conditions dictated by a new perspective. The

sequence of Transformative learning activities is not made up of invariable developmental steps; rather, the activities should be understood as sequential moments of 'meaning becoming clarified.' (p.193)

The disorienting dilemma which prompted a new perspective at Allen School was a fight among several students and their angry parents. The students involved in the fight were suspended, and the parents of these students banded together to protest this disciplinary action. They accused the school administration of partiality and unfairness rather than addressing the issues with their children.

The angry parents' confrontations precipitated Allen's staff members to re-examine their goals and hopes for the educational process. We said to ourselves and in unison, "We do not want to live our lives this way. This is not our vision of what a school should be. The way it is, it's not worth it! Life has no meaning. We must do something or get out."

We acknowledged that students' negative behavior that was interfering with their learning process. We addressed the problem with a schoolwide character-building program, which was based upon caring and honoring differences and creating a "family" by involving everyone in the school. We learned how to "learn together" and, in the process of learning, transformed the school.

The following key elements were involved in the Allen School transformation:

Trust Relationships—Trust is something that cannot be demanded or legislated. It is something that must be earned and merited. And unless there is a healthy trust relationship between the principal and the teachers, any attempt to incorporate a character education program in the school is doomed to failure. In establishing and strengthening trust relationships, one needs to be genuinely interested in the well-being of others. We learned the value of recognizing each other's strengths and encouraging their usage on one hand, while acknowledging our weaknesses and supporting their development on the other.

Building trust also involves the creation of a safe, comfortable environment. We learned to think about the times that we felt like we belonged and were valued. We found it helpful to ask such questions as: What was the environment? Who was the leader? What did he/she do to create such an environment?

Courage to Change— Resistance to change is normal. And when one proposes to undertake a task of transformation, one is likely to meet resistance every step of the way. One who leads transformative changes in organizations must have the courage to change before he/she can encourage others to overcome their own resistances.

Introductions of new programs, or innovations to ongoing systems involve risk-taking. A prudent leader, or school principal, needs to identify a worthy objective—or a vision—that is not only worth the risk-taking, but attainable and self-fulfilling.

In the Allen Experience, the immersion of students in positive character traits, so that they might become better persons, impelled the teachers and school staff to find the courage to change as well.

Consensus Decision-Making— The role of the principal in elevating skills in consensus decision-making may be described as follows:

- The principal doesn't decide.
- The principal contributes ideas.
- The principal serves as a guide.
- The principal gets resources and/or resource persons.
- The principal provides factual information.

Trade-off is a necessary factor in consensus decision-making. The number of people making a decision determine the amount of time it will take. This process seals people's commitment to implement the decision.

Initiating a back-to-basics character-development program in an environment such as Allen requires the total commitment that consensus decision-making generates.

Team Building— Team cohesiveness is critical to the process of consensus decision-making. And the principal plays a key role in this respect. A team is more than just a group of people. It is a collection of individuals with different capabilities who think and move in one direction. To make the team effective, the principal must continually make the goal—or vision—come alive and relate to current issues. He must be a focused task director, allowing the members to disagree among themselves in order that they may arrive at the best possible agreement.

Brainstorming— One of the many useful ways to draw idea contributions from a team is brainstorming. At Allen, brainstorming sessions were held to involve the whole staff in the transformation process. The sharing of ideas and redesigning of the school environment resulted from the team's synergy.

At Allen, we employed brainstorming to serve as the foundation for other problem-solving techniques. We found it to be a helpful tool to separate creativity from analysis. The "Word of the Week," for which Allen is widely known, is the result of brainstorming. The various ways in which the program was cascaded to achieve maximum effectiveness are a result of brainstorming, too.

Brainstorming is an idea-generating tool and should not be misconstrued as a method to completely solve problems.

Valuing Process— Implementation of a positive character traits education program in school is far from mechanical. It is unlike the introduction of a new subject matter or new electronic teaching/learning aids for which competence is the key word. The immersion of students in basic values such as respect, responsibility, honesty, or patriotism becomes more a matter of instilling a sense of service in them rather than a measure of any teaching competency.

Consider the task of administering discipline. Before Allen's transformation, the teachers and the principal were primarily concerned about doing everything properly and enforcing the rules. After undergoing a valuing process—essentially a self-examination pondering on questions such as "What do I believe?" and "How should I act?"—the teachers and the principal identified their own value systems and prioritized them.

A shift from the value of "competence" to the value of "service" facilitated the character education process at Allen. The task of administering discipline became an opportunity to contribute to the betterment of society. The concern shifted from approval of actions by administrators to a concern about what is considered to be right for a better society.

Seeing Good in Others— This is a fundamental principle in the success of the character education program at Allen. The primary ethic of character education is to support the development of inherent goodness. We must be able to look into the soul, find the good, and then respond in a way that helps that goodness to surface.

The previous practice at Allen in dealing with misbehaving students was to define the misdeeds and impose punishments appropriate to the school's rules on the offenders, who were then expected to feel guilty. The principle of "seeing the good in others," however, restructured this practice. In dealing with misbehaving students, what is good about the student's personhood is emphasized over the student's offense.

"Were you not the one who helped Miss _____ carry her load of books the other day?" "I saw you last week pacifying two fighting kids. What motivated you to do that?" and similar questions precede a discussion of the reported offense.

It is important to help the student look at what is inherently good in himself/herself, as opposed to focusing solely on his/her misdeed. This approach allows the student to recognize that the "bad thing" he/she did was not the result of his/her being a "bad" person, but of a lapse in judgment, for which he/she would be willing to square off by accepting the penalty with courage, rather than with resentment.

The idea of seeing the good in others is hardly new. It goes back to ancient times described by Aristotle as a holistic view of a living being as form and matter, or body and soul. Tied into this concept of potentiality and actuality, students are like freshly sprouted seeds breaking through the soil. They contain a much greater potential than what is shown at first. The task of the modern school must be to cultivate a culture that is conducive to the growth of full potential in all students.

Effective Culture Change— In and of itself, cultural change indicates that everyone within the culture is making a change. Eating habits are part of one's culture, and making a change would be distressing. The same is true in changing a school's culture, such as what happens when students, teachers, staff, and principals take steps to transform their environment.

In the 1950s, home, school, and church were of the greatest influence to students. By the 1990s they were the least according to a Michigan State University 1990 study entitled "Influences on Young People."

Greatest Influence on Students

	1950	1970	1990
1.	Home	Home	Peers
2.	School	Peers	T.V./Media
3.	Church	T.V./Media	Home
4.	Peers	School	School
5.	T.V.	Church	Church

Initiating a back-to-basics character education program to regain the school's position as a significant influence on the students involves a change, or at the least, a reconfiguration of the school's current culture.

Empowering of Staff— One of the key steps in developing a character education program is empowering teachers to create a value system that they are committed to, one that will form the basis for character education.

Character education will only be as effective as the ability of the entire staff to model the desired values and traits. Empowerment means giving the teachers the time and responsibility to do the task.

At Allen, empowerment started with the creation of a core team that collected some basic data about the situation. They surveyed parents and teachers. The results were shared with the entire staff. A staff consensus was developed and the primary issue facing the school was identified. The teachers were then empowered to deal with it.

In-service time was granted to do this work on Tuesday and Thursday afternoons. Sessions were teacher-led, and among themselves, they discussed and shared their problems.

Understanding Systems View— A systems view is about seeing wholes and patterns of change. And a prerequisite for building character schoolwide begins with developing a systems perspective.

Allen's transformation began with a vision and the engagement of a broad-based effort of the constituents of the system. The goal was always understood and there were specific tasks, but it was not highly organized. The activities emerged and different people jumped in to provide leadership at various times.

A systems view is one that is filled with both realism and hope. It is a view that sees interrelated problems, but also sees a path for change and improvement. It is not an optimistic view, but one grounded in the reality of the present and with insight into the interacting issues that make up the whole.

Mapping a Course of Action— In establishing a school character education program, it is building the commitment to a vision and then creating the participatory structures for multiple actions to take place, rather than the normal process of setting goals and writing out detailed steps.

Early on in the transformation process, we engaged ourselves in skill-development processes where we learned about consensus decision-making and brainstorming. With these new skills, we set out literally to redesign the school environment. Within a year we began implementing new activities and weekly routines. We did not lock ourselves into a rigid formula, or simply copy another school's program, but continued to evolve the new environment. By the end of the second year, the new values had become second nature. We continued to be highly motivated. This was our program. We created it. It was congruent with our values system.

Being Positive; Keeping a Sense of Humor— Introducing a new program, especially one as controversial as character education, could result in a host of problems not normally germane to academic teaching. While most problems are overcome by excellent teamwork and prudent leadership, those that aren't can be lightened with an injection of witticism or humor. The times when things don't fall into place despite the best laid plans are the times when keeping the vision in focus and maintaining a positive point of view is so important.

Finally, after a year-long in-service on the elements of transformation, the staff finally decided to identify the character traits we wanted our students to be immersed in. Employing the skills learned in brainstorming and consensus decision-making, the staff, community leaders, parents and students came up with the following character traits:

Punctuality	Consideration
Promptness	Resourcefulness
Readiness	Tolerance
Responsibility	Uniqueness
Respectfulness	Citizenship
Obedience	Patriotism
Self-Control	Loyalty
Politeness	Courage
Truthfulness	Initiative
Honesty	Self-Reliance
Thankfulness	Perseverance
Kindness	Cleanliness
Generosity	Self-Discipline
Goodwill	Independence
Joyfulness	Neatness
Patience	Sportsmanship
Cooperation	Fairness
Helpfulness	Confidence

A course of study for each grade level and character trait was developed. Structuring the program was the next step in the transformation. The staff agreed that, if the students were to change, the environment in the school must change. It must be an environment different from what children experienced outside the school. The language in the building must change and the staff must serve as models and mentors in this new environment. The weekly process is as follows:

1. The Word of the Week is presented to the entire school on Monday by the principal. The character trait is defined and an example on how to emulate the trait is given.
2. During the homeroom period on Tuesday through Thursday, teachers spend five minutes of homeroom period discussing the character trait.
3. On Friday, the word is highlighted in a ten-minute assembly. Each week one of the homerooms is responsible for making a presentation on the Word of the Week.

After the first year of implementation, the staff felt the need to reach the parents. A flyer was developed for each character trait. It contained artwork developed by the students and references to classical books that parents could read to learn more about the character trait.

Another key element of the program is the parent contract. In this contract, the student agrees to abide by the school rules in attendance, punctuality, wearing the school uniform, following the code of student conduct, completing homework on time, and assuming responsibility for his/her own success.

The parents agree to provide a place and routine for study, and to insist on attendance, wearing the uniform, reinforcing the code of student conduct, completion of homework on time, reviewing and returning periodic reports, and participating in school activities.

The staff agrees to provide a disciplined, safe and structured learning environment, to enforce the code of student conduct, provide educational experiences with high expectations for every student, enforce academic standards, and communicate with parents on student progress.

This school year, to further strengthen the change in attitude, behavior and study habits, the staff at Allen is providing the students with experiences in applying what they have learned in real-life situations. Each grade level adopted a service project. Among the projects were:

- Clean-up and beautification of the school
- Serving as mentors of a multi-handicapped school
- Food for pantries
- Nursing home visits
- Senior citizen center activities
- Recycling projects

After the first two years of Allen's character education program, students' conduct improved remarkably. Students show better behavior, better attitudes and better study habits. Suspensions dropped dramatically, teacher absenteeism ceased to be a problem. By 1992, Allen had risen from 28th to 5th place in standardized California Achievement Tests. By 1995, Allen ranked number one in the district.

References

Joiner, Charles W. (Jr.), *Building Character Schoolwide: The Allen School Experience*. West Mifflin, PA. Your Environment, Inc., 1995,

Scott, Charles L., "Shaping Character," *The American School Board Journal*, 1992, Vol. 179. No. 12.28-30.